Brand Storm

Pearson Education

In an increasingly competitive world, it is quality of thinking that gives an edge. An idea that opens new doors, a technique that solves a problem, or an insight that simply helps make sense of it all.

We work with leading authors in the fields of management and finance to bring cutting-edge thinking and best learning practice to a global market.

Under a range of leading imprints, including Financial Times Prentice Hall, we create world-class print publications and electronic products giving readers knowledge and understanding which can then be applied, whether studying or at work.

To find out more about our business and professional products, you can visit us at www.business-minds.com

For other Pearson Education publications, visit www.pearsoned-ema.com

Pearson
Education

Brand Storm

A tale of passion, betrayal, and revenge

Will Murray

FINANCIAL TIMES

Prentice Hall

An imprint of **Pearson Education**

London · New York · San Francisco · Toronto · Sydney · Tokyo · Singapore
Hong Kong · Cape Town · Madrid · Paris · Milan · Munich · Amsterdam

Pearson Education

Head Office:
Edinburgh Gate, Harlow CM20 2JE
Tel: +44 (0)1279 623623 Fax: +44 (0)1279 431059

London Office:
128 Long Acre, London WC2E 9AN

Tel: +44 (0)20 7447 2000 Fax: +44 (0)20 7240 5771

Website: www.business-minds.com

First published in Great Britain in 2000
© Pearson Education Limited 2000

The right of Will Murray to be identified as Author of this Work has been asserted by him in accordance with the Copyright, Designs and Patents Act 1988.

ISBN 0 273 65095 5
British Library Cataloguing in Publication Data.
A CIP catalogue record for this book can be obtained from the British Library.

10 9 8 7 6 5 4 3 2 1

Design and artwork by Bora Marketing Communications Ltd.

Printed and bound in Italy by Rotolito Lombarda.

The Publishers' policy is to use paper manufactured from sustainable forests.

TO GEORGE & HENRY

Keep having clever, good ideas

Never hesitate to take action

Live your dreams

Be passionate, kind and true
in everything

British-born Will Murray is the founder of Team Murray, an ideas organisation that combines a love of new ideas and an understanding of human dynamics with a passion for servicing customers. As well as working on a number of business-related books, Will provides one-to-one coaching for companies wishing to express their love to their customers and immerse their brands in a customer service ethic.

Before founding Team Murray, Will was a 'Pathfinder' with the Fourth Room, a UK based strategic marketing consultancy, whose promise is to help you see today what you can be tomorrow.

After obtaining a degree in economics at Leicester University, Will went on to study advertising at Watford College, before starting his career at the sharp end of marketing with several leading UK retail companies. Will later joined British Telecom (BT) where, as Head of Business Marketing, responsible for BT's largest clients, he helped create one of the most competitive sales and service teams in one of the fastest moving markets in the world.

As Marketing Director at Ernst and Young, Will took on the challenge of transforming a firm accustomed to traditional recurring business to one competing daily for non-traditional new business where the individual partners must personify the firm's brand.

These experiences have established Will as one of the most experienced and innovative 'people marketers' in the world, which, combined with his inner belief in customer service, has been the inspiration for Brand Storm.

Will has two sons, George and Henry, lives in the country, and is an enthusiastic and passionate painter who loves modern art, interior landscaping and architecture.

CONTENTS

Will's book is a wonderful and exciting book to read. We need many more books like this, and rest assured they are coming our way.

Why? Because doing business on the Internet is hard, very hard, and it is a true battle for customer attention. A battle so intense that you might win it and lose it in the same year. A battle that you will have to fight and fight again and then fight once more. That old saying about losing battles to win the war will become the business norm as early as 2005.

We have seen networks before. The road network, the canal network, the rail network, the airline network and of course the telephone network to name but a few. But we have never seen an information and communications network on the scale of the Internet before.

By 2010 two billion people and close to 80 million companies will be trading on the Internet – all the time, in real time! Can you imagine it? I'm trying to every day. We call it a 24 x 7 economy. Do we really know what that is?

I believe that by 2030 the Internet will have created more jobs than there are people to do them, and that's allowing for the fact that today's six billion people will grow to perhaps ten billion by then.

One hundred million companies trading 24 hours a day, 7 days a week. Three shifts a day in every company. Three people for every job. Unbelievable! The world economy is currently around $30 trillion. Roughly one third is in the Americas, one third is in Europe and Africa, and one third is in Asia. Do you remember Orwell's *1984*?

In India and China, which doubtless will be the biggest economies by 2030, there will be over two billion people connected to the Internet. Today worldwide there are a little under 400 million. India and China will have five times the Internet economic output in their countries that we have today worldwide from those 400 million. These are phenomenal concepts just to place in your mind and consider for a moment. Will anyone dominate the Internet?

It might be possible that some companies like Yahoo! dominate it for a while. But it will only be for a while. The Internet is an ecosystem, it's biological, it's organic, it can't be outsmarted, it can't be ruled and it can't be dominated, at least not for long. It invokes democracy.

The battle for customer attention lies ahead for each and every one of us, whether we are Yahoo! or an organic farmer in Ohio. Whether we are a painter in Nepal or a wine grower in Tuscany. By 2030 the world will be a much more democratic place ... the Internet has guaranteed that single fact.

Get ready then to engross yourself in Will's book. Get your mind ready for the brand storm that's coming headlong straight at you like a juggernaut at night with its lights blazing and its horn blaring. Don't step in its way or attempt to board as it comes past. Try and stop it and it will run you down.

... Enjoy the ride.

Thomas Power
Chief Knowledge Officer,
The Ecademy.com
www.Ecademy.com
August 2000

APPLAUSE

The most exciting aspect of writing *Brand Storm* has been sharing the whole project with great people. I can't thank any of them too much.

David Turner has been fantastic from the start supporting me in both words and deeds. Thanks for your endless time and help David.

Beverly Mann has been brilliant spending hours with me developing the models and then reading draft copy through the night. Thanks for your ceaseless encouragement Beverly.

Piers Schmidt and the whole team at the Fourth Room who helped me to develop my ideas. Thanks, guys.

Richard James who showed great support for the project and introduced me to some superb people. Thanks Richard.

Richard Stagg at Financial Times Prentice Hall who is a star. Thanks, Richard, for the trust and sharing the vision.

Jacqueline Cassidy at Financial Times Prentice Hall who has been first class to work with. You're a fine editor. Thanks, Jacqueline.

Thomas Power, and all the dreamers, thanks.

Kevin Wolff at Financial Times Prentice Hall for building a storming website.

Mum and Dad for supporting me through thick and thin. Thanks, both of you.

Last, but definitely not least, George and Henry who make life a joy and are the best kids in the world. Thanks for being so special. I love you.

What the hell is going on, new media, virtual reality, Internet millionaires in their teens, dotcom grannies surfing the web? All pretty exciting stuff!

One thing is clear, if you have the imagination and the guts, this is the best time to be in business since the Industrial Revolution. Everything is up for grabs. Almost every rule is ready to be challenged. The Wild West meets the Swinging Sixties, which means many winners, more losers, many things working, while still more failing.

But hold your horses – there are a couple of rules that won't alter. One, human nature doesn't change and two, if you allow technology to dictate to you it's the road to hell. If you want proof of what happens when you ignore these rules, look at all the sixties' housing developments now being demolished as slum clearance.

It's this mix of irresistible forces and immovable objects that will make the next few years so exciting and has prompted me to write *Brand Storm*. So what does it all mean for companies, brands and their customers?

Over the next few years both you and your customers are going to have literally thousands of new choices to make. It is not being over dramatic to say that today's business infrastructure is going to be blown apart. 'Market cyclones' will rip into markets – your markets – devastating the status quo.

Underneath all today's excitement lies a harsh fact. Your markets are going to go on growing at an average rate or maybe, if you are really lucky, two or three times what you experience today. On the other hand, increasing ease of global market entry means new suppliers hunting your customers. And, new suppliers are going to keep on coming and coming. Forget all the cyberspace hype for a second, your customers are going to be under siege.

In tomorrow's world only extreme performers by today's standards will survive. For these extreme performers immersing their whole operation in their brand will be their differentiater.

But this is not the whole picture or indeed even the most important part. The most dramatic repercussion of the Internet concerns not companies but people. It is not the Internet that is important but the fact that it heralds a new age: the human age. Get prepared for empowered consumers and global consumer champions.

This is why the book is called *Brand Storm: A tale of passion, betrayal and revenge*. The next few years will see the birth of both passionate organisations and passionate consumers. The trust of some of those consumers is going to be betrayed and their revenge will be swift and terrible.

Enter *Brand Storm*, introducing a new way of looking at customers, the marketing mix and brand definitions. Brand storm will help you identify your corporate psyche and develop a living brand constitution, the impact of which you can actually measure, review and audit.

To make it easy to follow, *Brand Storm* is divided into three scenes: ideas, actions and dreams.

'Ideas' explains step-by-step the philosophy of *Brand Storm* from the Internet phenomenon through to the human economy, market conditions, customer responses, customer service strategies and from brand evolution to the vital importance of corporate integrity, self-actualisation, and corporate karma. (If the last bit sounds esoteric, get it wrong and you'll be punished by vociferous consumers and competitors.)

Tomorrow's companies will be exposed to the same rigorous examination that today's politicians face. Like today's politicians, any lack of integrity will be exposed and punished.

Brand Storm is designed not just to be read, but to be *worked*. This is where the next scene, 'Actions', comes in. In conjunction with our Internet site, www.brandstorm.com, *Brand Storm* has been designed as your gateway to a supportive, brand storming experience. Management consultancy without the consultants. Each of the phases within 'Actions', has clear steps, is supported by the Internet site and is measurable. My intention is to compel, motivate and empower you to brand storm your own organisation.

Brand Storm is designed not just to be read, but to be *worked* – management consultancy without the consultants

The last scene, 'Dreams', is all about motivation and inspiration. If you can't dream, you can't embrace life. 'Dreams' collects together personal insights and aspirations from people who have thought about the human economy and asked themselves what it means. They inspired me; I hope they inspire you.

Personally, I love working with people, organisations and brands. I hope that through the *Brand Storm* website. I will get to know some of you and be able to share your thoughts, experiences, findings, and successes as you implement *Brand Storm*.

You might wonder what motivates someone to write a book like this. Well, over the past 12 years, I have been immersed in making companies succeed by living their brands; initially at BT, working with literally thousands of sales and service personnel and then as Marketing Director at Ernst and Young in the UK. Recently at the Fourth Room and with Team Murray, I have applied the spirit of *Brand Storm* and I know it works.

There is nothing more exciting than being involved in an organisation that is doing something exceptional, where your customers adore you and the staff are really buzzing. Yet, good examples are few and far between. This shouldn't be the case and maybe the approaching tidal wave of choice will remove the apathy and contentment that exists in too many of today's organisations.

I also wanted to challenge the traditional business book formula. Books in many sectors have moved on much faster than business books, which have become stuck in a rut. Most of today's gardening, cookery or interior design books compel you to take action. Just picking them up and browsing is a joy; they are a riot of fantastic colour and appealing illustrations. They are genuinely inspirational and even if you don't actually follow their ideas to the letter they foster your interest in the subject and inspire you to develop your own ideas.

That is what I want to achieve with *Brand Storm*. A business book that is emotionally engaging, accessible and actionable and that leads to people changing their organisation's fortunes. I hope you enjoy reading *Brand Storm* and that you start enjoying business again.

Business should be fun.

Good luck, and I'm looking forward to hearing from you.

Will Murray

will.murray@brandstorm.com

If you never dream, you'll never embrace life

Wishbones

In the spirit of doing as I suggest others do I am including my own *Brand Storm* wishbone in the book. So what do I mean by a wishbone?

A wishbone to me should be a plain English blueprint for the success of your idea. It should be the elixir of life for your venture, containing all the unique DNA needed for your future success.

Why call it a wishbone? At the stage you write it, that is all that it.

To turn a wishbone into a backbone you have to action it.

This is the spirit that drove me to create the *Brand Storm* wishbone. To me *Brand Storm* was an exciting new business venture that could quite easily have been diverted all over the place and quickly lost its way. Creating the *Brand Storm* wishbone has been essential, both in framing my objectives for the book, and in holding the whole production team on the same track.

I have decided to include it in the book partly as a live example to illustrate the text, partly to foster transparency of my own actions and partly because you, as customers, have a right to know.

The Brand Storm wishbone

Vision

Business success in the new human economy, through mutual trust.

BHAG (big hairy audacious goal)

To be the first truly emotionally engaging, enjoyable, and accessible business book.

Purpose

To help you, my customers, establish economically viable and sustainable trust with your customers, regardless of how you trade with them.

Promise

To enhance your future business prospects in an enjoyable and memorable way.

Approach

To illuminate the future, not just describe it.
To make the ideas actionable, not just fascinating.
To inspire you to want to live your own dreams.

Strategy

To ignite you to take positive action by appealing to your emotions as well as your reason. To help you implement *Brand Storm* through the dedicated website. To encourage dialogue between you and the author and between you and other readers, to create an ongoing and shared experience.

Tactics

Make it fun. Make it simple. Make it visual. Make it dynamic. Make it doable.

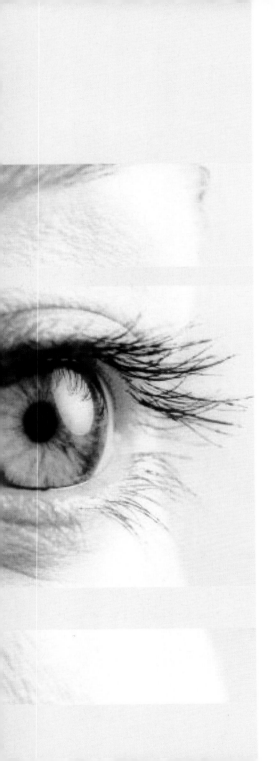

Brand Storm values

→ Openness

→ Fairness

→ Passion

→ Belief

→ Humanity

→ Hope

Brand Storm virtues

→ Insight

→ Imagination

→ Illumination

→ Inspiration

→ Ignition

→ Involvement

Brand Storm visuals

→ Use colour strongly

→ Use space wisely

→ Use simplicity

→ Use emphasis powerfully

→ Illustrate often

Brand Storm voice

→ Open

→ Irreverent

→ Parabolic

→ Joyous

Dictionary definition of open:

Not shut, exposing the interior, unobstructed, uncovered, accessible, available, not enclosed, ready to receive, free to be discussed, unconcealed, undisguised, generous, spread out, unrestricted, not dense, clear, unfrozen, not hazy, frank, unreserved, exposed to view, to speak out, to begin, to cordially welcome, ready to receive and consider new ideas; open-eyed, open-handed, open-minded, open book.

Characters in order of appearance

The audience

- Dependent customers – looking for satisfaction
- Free customers – looking for delight
- Liberated customers – looking for love

The stars

- Performance brands – offering satisfaction
- Personality brands – offering delight
- Partner brands – offering love

The impresarios

- Benefit firsts – delivering performance brands
- Flexible friends – delivering personality brands
- People companies – delivering partner brands

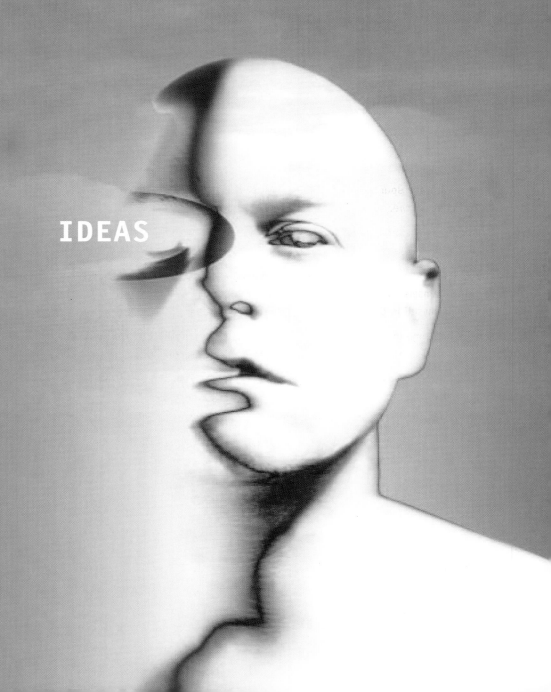

Scene one

IDEAS

IDEAS

Anyone with any spunk must find it is impossible to think about the next few years with anything less than a tidal wave of excitement and a sense of awe.

It is not just change, because change is now a way of life. It is the fact that the next few years will be a raw, heartbreaking, gut-wrenching adventure.

The last time I felt like this was reading adventure books as a child; saving doomed comrades, cracking codes, defeating pirates and rescuing damsels in distress was all in a day's work. Using my imagination, I become a hero, overcoming fantastic odds. And by immersing myself in the adventure, it all became real. I beat those villains, defeated the enemy, and won the rescued damsels' hearts.

For the first time in my adult life, fiction has become fact again. Now anyone can be James Bond or even Superman. Make up your own rules, overturn the odds and create a world every bit as exciting as any child's adventure.

This is a truly magical time to live in, and those with the belief, stamina, and vision will create their own magic worlds. If your imagination is strong enough and your partners are as up for it as you are, then go for it. It doesn't matter whether you are leaving school, experiencing a mid-life crisis, or were previously contemplating a gentle slide into retirement; *now* is the time of your life.

The only difference between being a child reading an adventure book and being an adult in the 21st century is that the child can put the book down, and you can't.

Fiction has become fact. Now anyone can be James Bond or even Superman

King Arthur, come on down

But if you want to enter this magic kingdom, don't rely on the same tried and tested ideas and approaches that have been used over the last few years.

This is no time for the faint hearted, the business style and business ethics of the last century will no longer provide the dividends that they have so far delivered. For a better guide we have to travel much further back in time.

King Arthur and his Round Table have more chance of making it big in the 21st century than most of today's business tycoons. Over the next few years, the types of quality so much admired in King Arthur's day will come back into fashion. Come back honour, chivalry, respect, integrity, purpose, and bravery. Better informed, more discerning customers are going to be far more demanding about the type of service they require. And, they will have the means to take action in the face of dissatisfaction.

Levels of information about corporate behaviour available in the public domain will cut down dishonest brands. Global choice will drown the mediocre. Solutions created by individuals, rather than created for them by market analysis, are about to kick traditional marketing into touch.

There is no turning the clock back; no stopping the bus because you want to get off. With the choices available to you, there is no reason why you would want to. You are about to get greater lifestyle freedom coupled with greater commercial muscle than ever before. Even someone working at home, on their own, can address and market to a global audience. Anything Microsoft or McDonald's can do, you can do, too.

King Arthur has more chance of making it big in the 21st century than most of today's business tycoons

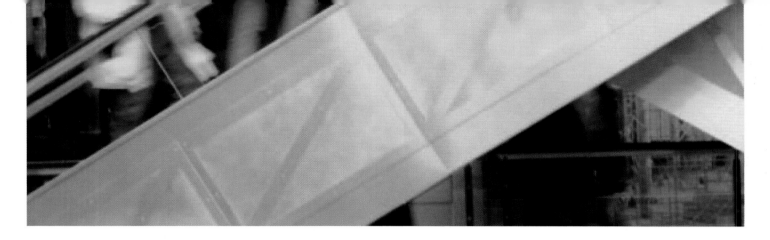

Ideas 'r' us

Split into several takes, 'Ideas' is a journey from Internet to identity, designed to stir the imagination of anyone even vaguely interested in the business of satisfying customers.

It does not matter whether you are an entrepreneur, wannabe entrepreneur, company manager, professional, big city corporate type or even a society pacesetter, there will be something in 'Ideas' to help you make your bit of the earth move.

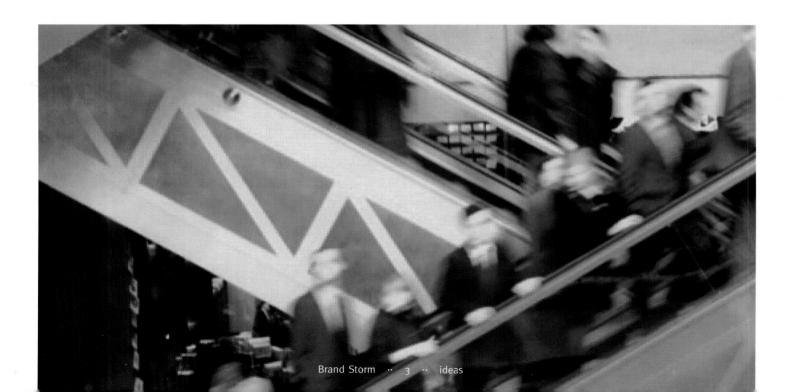

One man one voice

The story of the internet

Universal suffrage, or everyone having a vote, is the cornerstone of the western democratic world. Much energy and oceans of blood have been spent by a great many people over the years to establish a way of life which many of us now take for granted.

What we are about to experience is a phenomenon no less powerful than political democracy that will amaze people today as much as being dropped into the 21st century would amaze a medieval peasant.

Universal commercial suffrage

The Internet is about to extend universal suffrage beyond the political domain into the economic world. One man one vote is about to become one man one voice.

Universal commercial suffrage will be massive. Most of what we have seen so far is really a game. Old world people using a new world tool to play old world games. And why wouldn't they? People with power today won't upset the established commercial order just as the kings, nobles, and ruling classes were never over keen on democracy.

Just as elections have given people a say in politics so the Internet will give people a say in commerce. For the first time in history, people in the western world and eventually in the entire world are going to have a medium for openly expressing their views about the companies that dominate their lives. They will be able publicly to rebuke the commercial aristocracy and bureaucrats who have ruled them with a rod of iron for the last 150 years. And not only will they be able to have their say, they will be able to rise up and take action.

All this without any revolutions and bloodshed – truly remarkable.

1

One man one vote will become one man one voice

Anyone who supports democracy should be celebrating in the streets, and, if they still have one, throwing their hat in the air. When we look back at the start of the 21st century and the economic birth of the Internet, the commercial enfranchisement of the general public will turn out to be the internet's most significant contribution to our lives.

The slow birth of democracy

The evolution of democracy has taken thousands of years in the process, it has changed the face of politics and subsequently, our whole society, creating the world as we know it today. The emergence of modern democracy in post-classical Europe has been marked by four major phenomena.

First the establishment of free government and the right of a country to rule itself. In Britain it started with Magna Carta in 1215, and took a civil war and the execution of a king; in France they needed a revolution. We both got there in the end even if our early parliaments didn't bear much comparison with life today. This brings me to the second major socio-political phenomenon.

The step-by-step establishment of universal suffrage and the abolition of slavery and apartheid. Everyone winning the vote has been as hard to achieve as the concept of power sharing in the first place. Every extension of the vote has been a hard-fought, drawn-out battle, leading to the Suffragette movement and the American War of Independence among other things. The battle still rages around the world as witnessed by the abolition of apartheid in South Africa some years ago.

The First and Second World War comprise the third phenomenon. Nation fought nation with millions dying to preserve independence and freedom for all. The two bloodiest wars of all time shook the whole world as the very concept of democracy was put to the test. Luckily for all of us, but at a horrific cost, democracy won the day.

The last phenomenon, behavioural transparency, hasn't been as dramatic or as bloody as the first three but has had as much impact on today's political scene. Kings and politicians used to be able to say pretty much one thing and do whatever they liked, ask Henry the Eighth. Not so today, as Prince Charles will tell you after the recent Princess Diana episode.

In the UK it can be traced back at least to the Profumo affair in the 1960's when the press took their boxing gloves off and the private lives of politicians became public. In the USA the latest Clinton debacle is proof that it is alive and well. Screw up in private and be hounded in public. Behavioural transparency is now a way of life for political and public figures.

Screw up in private and be hounded in public

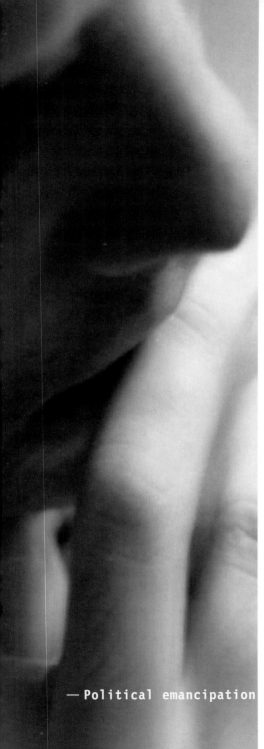

A hundred to one

Commercial emancipation, no less a task in order of magnitude with its associated, socio-economic upheaval, is about to happen in less than ten years, one hundredth of the time.

So what exactly is happening, and why is this aspect of the Internet going to be so overwhelmingly important?

Well, a number of things are going to happen simultaneously ...

The right of reply

This is the cornerstone of our new commercial democracy. For the first time ever, every single person in the advanced world is going to have a chance to have his or her say. No more writing to the papers, no more trying to get on TV, no more writing to your MP, and no more writing to companies with your complaint only to be ignored.

Got something to say? Get on the Internet and get it out there. If the company you want to talk to won't talk to you, go direct to their customers, their partners, and their shareholders. Not everyone will hear you but the important ones will. People won't do business with a company without checking it out on the net first, searching both formal and informal sites.

—Political emancipation took 1,000 years, economic emancipation will take just ten —

New world order

In the days of the divine right of kings, a country's whole infrastructure revolved around the royal court. The introduction of government by the people saw the slow but continual development of a new political infrastructure. Out went the robber barons with their local fiefdoms and in came a new system of political parties with national, regional, and local representation. In came lobbying and pressure groups, and the whole political paraphernalia we know and love today, complete with anarchists and terrorists.

Just as happened for the political world so will it happen for the commercial world. Whole new global, customer-centric organisations are about to spring up. Like political parties but grouped around consumer interests, some will be profit making, some driven purely by interested parties keen to be heard, some will be peripheral but some will have real teeth and will bring down entire corporations.

The closest comparison we have today is the trade union movement. They provide a good example of just how powerful a force these new global consumer champions are set to be. These new consumer organisations are going to be huge. Do you want one breathing down your neck?

Power to the people

The power of the aristocracy was always based on land ownership. With a vast proportion of land owned by a few families, power was highly concentrated. Over the last 150 years following the Industrial Revolution, a new breed of industrial magnate appeared with a stranglehold on the new methods of manufacturing and wealth production. The dukes and earls of old became the industrial magnates of yesterday who went on to become the global company chairman and chief executives of today.

The one thing they all had in common was a monopoly on power. In each era, power was concentrated in a few hands. All this is set to change.

—————— Do you want a global consumer champion breathing down your neck? ——————

Giant, all-encompassing monoliths are facing a two-pronged attacked. The Internet is making entry into business easier than ever before. Barriers to entry are tumbling; every home now has the potential to be a global headquarters. Coupled with this is the public exposure of companies' private behaviour fuelling the requirement for corporate integrity and adherence to a set of clear beliefs. The increasing determination of people to establish their individuality is favouring the little man.

These trends are coming together to promote a new generation of small businesses and micro-entrepreneurs taking a slice of the corporate cake. Outside the fields of primary production and manufacturing where scale is still critical there – little major companies can offer that small ones can't. Yet, increasingly, there are many services and personality-based benefits that small companies are far better equipped to deliver.

Chain reaction

Ease of communication and virtual interaction are facilitating the growth of the networked economy. This doesn't just mean traditional companies talking to each other more; it means whole new dialogues and relationships.

Virtually every existing commercial relationship is being, or is about to be, challenged. New niches for fast, effective companies to exploit are being prised out of the hands of existing incumbents on a daily basis. Value chains are becoming far more complicated with traditional channel masters being knocked off their perches.

Disintermediation is opening up previously exclusive realms and markets for new players democratising previously monopolistic industries. The length of value chains from primary production to customer is increasing, but becoming less a production driven chain and more of a web revolving around the consumer.

Here today, global tomorrow

If you are in business today, you might as well be global. Ok, it is not quite as simple as that for everyone. The issues of establishing global points of presence in the real world are the same as ever. But for a small company putting its toe in the water, it has never been easier. If a virtual presence is all you need, then you are laughing.

———— Every home is now a potential global headquarters ————

Until recently global was synonymous with big. Not any more. The small, yet global, corporation is now set to become a reality. Highly focused companies will exploit the global audiences being delivered by the Internet and provide specialists with a scope never before possible.

With an increasing number of Internet-facilitated organisations providing services to a global audience, we will soon also see an entirely new type of company.

Set up to love the customers of remote Internet companies, 'customer guardians' will provide a physical point of presence in remote locations on an agency basis. Not necessarily involved in the initial sales or physical distribution process, 'customer guardians' will be set up from scratch with the right culture to provide unbelievably good customer service on behalf of the companies they represent within the customer's chosen location. Just watch this space, this will soon be one of the fastest growing business sectors in the world.

Time travel

Time to market has never been shorter. Fleetness of foot is the most important quality in a company today. No company will ever exploit a market 100 percent. Moving in and moving on will be the order of the day. This is why having a strong reputation that you can port with you as you browse across different opportunities will be critical to success.

Time for some serious grovelling

So how will it feel to be a customer in this new world compared to the way it feels today? Hard to put it into words but it will be so different. If you saw the movie *Pretty Women*, you will remember the scene where Julia Roberts goes shopping for the second time, this time with Richard Gere, and experiences serious grovelling. Now, you're getting the picture.

Customer guardians will soon be loving your customers

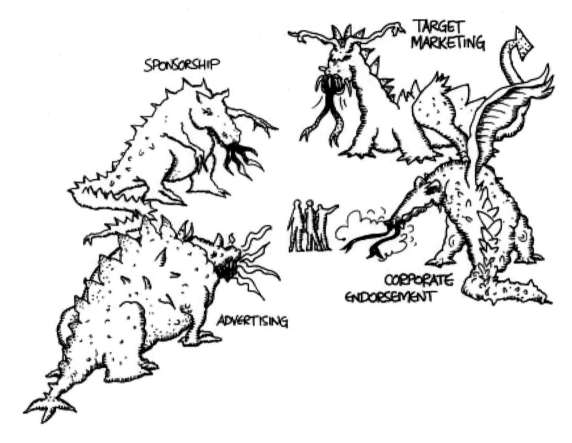

Today's customer experience

In today's world the whole system is still commerce centric with customers seen as targets. All today's retail-related language backs this up, price wars, target markets, target profiles, etc. Advertising, endorsements, and sponsorships are the main commercial weapons. Today's customers are just food for corporate dragons.

As a customer today you are just dragon fodder

Tomorrow's picture looks very different

Instead of having corporate sand thrown in their face the new consumer can flex their muscles or if that fails call on their pals to help them get what they want.

As a company tomorrow you won't be judged on what you say but what you do

The Internet is the cornerstone of consumer democracy with one customer one voice.

Expect customers that express their views loudly.

Customer 'unions' will magnify your customers' power.

Word of mouth will be the new advertising.

Treat behavioural transparency as a way of life.

Use customer guardians to love your customers.

Stop thinking about how the Internet can help you. Start thinking about delighting your customers.

KICKER:

The Internet isn't about companies; it's about enfranchised customers.

SCENE ONE
TAKE TWO

The human economy

Forget the Internet, forget technology, and forget shopping! Wake up to the human economy!

To see what I mean, let's slip back in time again, but this time go even further back. Our history has been a series of evolutionary stages, starting quite a few years ago with some sort of bang. What did or didn't happen in the first hundred million years or so remains a bit of a mystery. With opinion divided, let's not worry about that and look instead at the past hundred thousand years.

In the history of the world, man is just a blink of a planet-sized eye

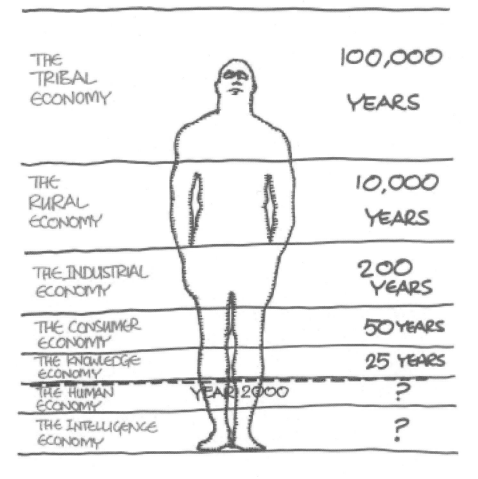

THE TRIBAL ECONOMY	100,000 YEARS
THE RURAL ECONOMY	10,000 YEARS
THE INDUSTRIAL ECONOMY	200 YEARS
THE CONSUMER ECONOMY	50 YEARS
THE KNOWLEDGE ECONOMY	25 YEARS
THE HUMAN ECONOMY	?
THE INTELLIGENCE ECONOMY	?

YEAR 2000

The seven ages of man

If you combine looking back at the last hundred thousand years, with a look forward to the next 20 to 30, you can split man's development into seven ages.

The tribal economy – 100,000 years plus

This period lasted quite a long time; the emphasis was on staying alive with lots of fighting wild animals and dragging women around by the hair. Must have been a tough old life, with not many home comforts. Domestication was definitely limited, but regional variations in speed of development would have been marked, with faster development where the climate made life easier, allowing people to concentrate on things other than survival.

People started to acquire possessions with basic tools, jewellery and clothes becoming popular. Even a bit of painting was going on. Someone, somewhere was writing a slate on the Flint Revolution.

The rural economy – 10,000 years or so

Things were definitely looking up by this stage. The emphasis shifted from staying alive to civilisation. Agriculture was starting to buzz, less hunting and fishing, more farming and shooting. People began to create surplus resources; specialisation and trading got going. Towns and cities shot up with religion growing in popularity. Nations were born.

Again this economy lasted pretty well – about 10,000 years give or take a few regional differences. What were the most memorable moments? I guess the construction of some fabulous buildings and the introduction of religious persecution stand out.

The industrial economy – a mere 200 years

So, on to the Industrial Revolution. With the introduction of machines, life took a new tack. The growth of towns and cities was ferocious; agriculture became less manual with people swapping the plough for the production line.

— Agriculture was starting to buzz, less hunting and fishing, more farming and shooting —

For the upper classes industrial production began to replace land as the primary source of wealth but for the working classes things were still hard. Instead of working yourself to death in a field you could now do it a factory. The gulf between rich and poor was as great as ever.

Did the industrial economy have a soul? It is hard to tell. Novelty and science came to the fore. The rate of change began substantially to quicken and people began to fall in love with the concept of speed and size. Speed applied to everything: manufacturing, travel, thinking, and doing. Size to buildings and empires. The industrial economy gave birth to the nouveau riche and rampant middle classes. The emphasis was on education, challenge, and achievement in every field, pushing back the boundaries and beating the hell out of anyone who got in your way.

The consumer economy – a trivial 50 years

Two world wars acted as an endnote to the industrial economy as nations put their newly manufactured toys to the test and tried to kill each other.

At the end of the Second World War, there was a bit of a pause while people got their breath back followed by a hearty lunge into consumerism. Mass gratification was born, not with each other in the Roman sense, but from buying things. The disposable society was at last here. Production changed to mass production and fashion became a dominant force in society.

Shopping became a serious pastime with shops packed full of groovy new things, affordable by the masses for the first time. Taste took a bit of a back seat, however, culminating in platform shoes, flared trousers, and shaggy perms. There were exceptions to these fashion disasters, however, like the Mini and the miniskirt, both of which caused a fair number of traffic accidents.

Ordinary people started to expect a life, before, not just after, they retired. Packaged foreign holidays took off big time. Although taken for granted now, package holidays were a major force in broadening people's horizons.

Mass gratification was born, not with each other in the Roman sense; but from buying things

At the start of the consumer economy emphasis was on fast moving consumer goods together with consumer durables like tvs. Pop music, television, and advertising became the dominant forces in society with traditional influences like law and order and respect for your elders evaporating. Sexual emancipation, personal freedom, and free expression were the order of the day.

By the end of the consumer economy most of these things were well established and a more holistic personal lifestyle idiom took root. A combination of all the things that had emerged at the start of the consumer economy, lifestyle living saved people the trouble of too much thinking by packaging together ready-made experiences.

Considering that yuppies (young upwardly mobile professionals) were a highlight of the consumer economy you might think it did pretty well lasting 50 years.

The knowledge economy – a transient 25 years

Getting up to date brings us to the knowledge economy. It reminds me a lot of the industrial economy, lots of rushing around challenging things because they can be challenged. The overt hedonism of the 1980's and the Thatcher gladiators have given way to feng shui self-enlightenment. Goodbye braces, hello body art.

There is a view that the pursuit of knowledge, like the pursuit of inventiveness, is an end in itself but I think history will prove otherwise. At any time of great progress in technology that progress will always dominate society for a time. So it is now with the Internet. Never has a technology had more airplay. What started as an interest for nerds has quickly become hyper-sexy.

Items worthy of comment so far in the knowledge economy have been the creation of Bill Gates and management consultants deciding casual wear is trendy.

But as the industrial age was a precursor of the consumer age so the knowledge economy is leading rapidly to the human one.

The overt hedonism of the 1980's and the Thatcher gladiators have given way to feng shui self-enlightenment

The human economy – number of years?

So what is the human economy? Why is it different and how long will it last?

The Industrial Revolution led to the consumer economy by creating the means of mass production. The knowledge revolution will lead to the human economy through the Internet. Mass production meant products for all, the Internet means power to all. It's simple really. The Internet destroys the monopoly on communication and global co-operation that has been the exclusive domain of governments and big companies. It is not just the power that this gives individuals that counts but the power of individuals to form and reform constantly changing human organisms.

The human economy switches power from essentially static governments and commercial organisations to organic human amoeba that will swarm around any issue they like to generate a global voice or, in some cases, global screams with the minimum of fixed infrastructure.

The implications for companies are as major as they are for governments and for society in general. Responsiveness and service levels will have to reach levels never before even contemplated to match these fast moving consumers and consumer groups. Traditional structures will not stand up to the wear and tear they are about to face. Companies must re-examine their organisations, their external relationships, and their structures to fit the human economy.

Consumers, too, will have a lot of adjusting to do as they encounter freedom for the first time. Like captive animals released into the wild they will take time to find their feet.

Exactly what life will be like in the human economy only time will tell, but compared to life in the knowledge economy it should be pretty wild. Get together with whom you like about whatever you like. Create a consumer group to last only a few weeks if that is what is required. See and talk to anyone about anything from the comfort of your own home or even walking around in the street. Challenge the stock exchange, challenge government, set up a new company, create a new charity, all in co-operation with a wealth of other like-minded humans.

——————— Organic human amoeba will swarm around any issue to generate global screams ———————

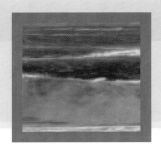

So, how fundamental a step is the human economy, compared to, say, the consumer or knowledge economy, and how long will it last?

I don't think that the human economy is the last step in the chain by a long way but it would appear to be more significant than the last few steps. History, however, is not on its side. If you look at the length of time previous stages have lasted, they tell a clear story: change is speeding up and economies are getting shorter, dramatically so.

A hundred thousand years for the first economy, down to 10,000, down again massively, this time to 200 years, followed by 50 years and 25 years for the knowledge economy. On this principle it should only last 10 to 15 years before the next economy rolls in.

Somehow I can't see it, though. There is something special about the human economy. Power is moving from politics to people and companies to consumers. This will take time but may result in less 'progress for the sake of progress' and a little more common sense.

What will make the human economy special? Human organisms that make the earth move.

The intelligence economy – number of years? Not a clue

Just as previous economies have had a destination so does the human economy, even if it is unclear how long it will take to get there. Changes in medical science, and, in particular, genetics will be the key. Link these to developments in virtual reality and destruction of the environment, and it is not hard to see a world where intelligence, both artificial and real, takes over from the physical world we know today.

———— What will make the human economy special? Human organisms that make the earth move ————

Back on earth as we know it, however, one can see how emphasis has shifted in society over the years. Building on Maslow's hierarchy of motivations for individuals you can create an economic hierarchy of motivations for society.

Murray's hierarchy of economic motivation

If you want to prosper in the human economy, you must understand and respect individualism not just pay lip-service to it. Today's market is about to become a very different place.

TRIBAL ⟶ SURVIVAL

RURAL ⟶ CIVILISATION

INDUSTRIAL ⟶ LEARNING

CONSUMER ⟶ LIFESTYLE

KNOWLEDGE ⟶ COMMUNICATION

HUMAN ⟶ INDIVIDUALITY

INTELLIGENCE ⟶ BEING

SNAPSHOT

The fabric and focus of today's knowledge economy is about to be replaced by a new human economy.

Power is shifting from companies to consumers.

Enter the world of fast moving consumer groups.

Existing commercial and political infrastructure will be challenged hard.

Traditional corporate structures won't stand the new wear and tear.

Individualism is the new mantra.

Future success isn't about tweaking what you are doing. It is about diametric change.

KICKER:

The human economy will feast on today's economic ecosystem.

SCENE ONE
TAKE THREE

3

Storm clouds
Welcome to the death zone!

Having established just how radical a shake-up is on its way, what are the implications for a company or organisation operating in today's market place?

To start with, let's get a few things straight.

It doesn't matter what you call it: the Internet revolution, the human economy, the networked economy, the wired world, the e-gang. They all describe the same phenomenon, and it's coming at you.

Regardless of where you are in the world, the real impact of this revolution is still to hit. To put things into context, thinking about the impact of the Internet today is like a toddler at play school thinking about what they want to read at university.

So what are the timescales?

Most of what you have seen so far has been for fun, which is great. Quite a few bright, far sighted people have made some cash and the rest of us have had an extra dimension added to our lives. The last ten years have been the fun zone with very little downside-only opportunity.

The next few years are going to be the love zone. Now is the time to get your act together, the games are over. Coming to terms with the Internet is not an option; there is no opt-out clause. Whatever business you are in, it's time both to integrate the Internet into your thinking and start offering serious service value. If you don't embrace every new idea and every new opportunity you can to make your customers love you more than they do your competitors, you're dead.

If you don't put yourself in the **driving seat,** you're going to be road kill

By mid-2003 we will be entering the death zone. Why the death zone? Because a lot of companies are going to die. Eighty percent of the skills required in the human economy reside in less than 20 percent of the people. You may have 10 or 20 years' success under your belt, but Antonia down the road is far cuter, five times as fit, knows more people than you do, is better informed, is mad for your customers and loads of people want to give her the cash she needs. Oh, and by the way, did I mention that she actually believes in what she is doing and has recruited a team that shares her dreams?

In the human economy you can forget about real world companies versus dotcoms, soon there will be just growth companies and ex-companies. If you don't put yourself in the driving seat, you're going to be road kill. And you haven't got long.

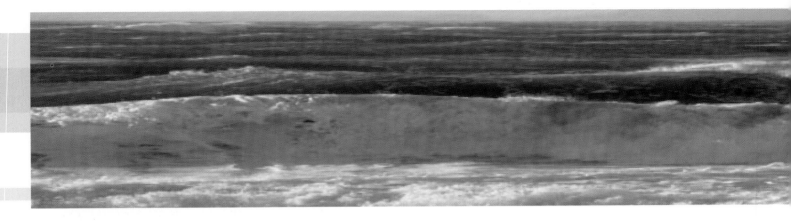

Storm warning

Market cyclones will sweep through established markets. These won't just change the rules, they will throw out the rulebook. If I were a weather forecaster rather than a business pundit, I'd be issuing a severe storm warning.

It is quite easy to make sweeping predictions about the future which sound scary but what are the underlying trends that are making these things a reality? Let's look at some of them.

Infinite choice

Choice, for better and worse, is now part of our everyday lives. Not just choice about what to buy but increasingly how to buy it. If you wanted to buy a car a few years ago, life was easy. If you wanted a new car you went to a main dealer or two and negotiated the best price you could. If you wanted a second-hand car you went to a second-hand car dealer. Not so today. You can import from overseas, buy direct on the web, buy pre-registered, use a supermarket, buy at auction. In fact main dealers are becoming your last resort.

And it is not just cars. Everything is going this way: tickets, clothes, information, in fact anything. The traditional retail distribution network is in distress. Manufactures are starting to experiment with direct sales; retailers and retail services are closing their branches.

Infinite choice is becoming a reality. People now have so many decisions to make it is becoming stressful. Every time I go shopping and don't use one of my millions of loyalty cards I get guilt. And when I've spent my money and got my points, more stress as I file all my statements, and decide how to spend the points. And it gets worse: even more guilt when I turn out my wallet, and find all the expired money-off vouchers I forgot to use.

Buying decisions are taking longer and longer to make as you research the varied options open to you. And if you don't, still more guilt because you know you are wasting money.

Big mistake

At the moment many companies are using technology to exploit temporary market advantage and make cost savings, such as closing branches and shops; not because they are not needed or wanted but for short-term gain and their own convenience. This is a big mistake. Actually, it's a huge mistake.

Companies that do this are signing their own death warrant. This is such a dangerous game and will result in some very big names going to the wall before you can say customer service. If you don't make your customers' lives easier while you still can, they will never, ever forgive you, and their revenge will be sweet. Just watch and see.

Superb information access

Information today is starting to become like sand in a desert – it is everywhere. Although this is rather like a double-edged sword, some things have to get worse before they get better. The Internet is both providing unprecedented levels of information to people and making traditional media companies more efficient. Over the next few years access to this information, via advanced info sorting techniques and search engines, will start to see real value being provided to consumers.

As described in 'One man one voice', organisations are springing up to help consumers sort out the wheat from the chaff when it comes to competitive offers. Price and value comparisons will soon be available for most product areas from personal finance to tvs and everything in between. With directly comparable, real time price comparisons for products and services, even for services that are priced to be deliberately confusing such as mobile phone services, companies are going to have to be far more imaginative to attract, and keep, customers.

But the most important factor when it comes to the growth of information about companies will be the informal groups that are about to spring up to review corporate behaviour. Anyone with either an interest in, or a grudge against, your company or your products is going to be given a chance to air their views.

If you don't start making your customers' lives easier while you still can,
they will never, ever forgive you

Sophisticated Internet sites and chat rooms, set up by technically expert individuals, will give consumers the chance to say whatever they like and people are going to want to hear. You've got a problem with your car, why not tell millions of people about it. You're thinking of buying a certain car, don't you want to know what the user club thinks? All those companies offering poor service and refusing to honour guarantees and warranty claims because of technicalities, beware! Your customers are about to have a field day. A tale of passion, betrayal, and revenge!

This is real power: when a company lets you down, don't get mad get even. People love sharing customer service horror stories with their friends and now it won't have to be just their friends. For the guy on the street, this is dream ticket. Think your company can just carry on the way it does today? Hah, welcome to the living nightmare. For instance, most of today's banks are going to have to look to their laurels, that's for sure, and we're not just talking convenience, we're talking morals.

Unlimited supply of products and services

The range of product choice available to consumers is going to be staggering. Virtually every manufacturer in the world is going to find a way of either directly or indirectly marketing their products almost everywhere in the world.

The potential choice for consumers would be totally bewildering without the help of consumer unions and customer guardians (predicted in Scene One). Marketing in tomorrow's world is going to be both tricky and exciting, with limitless opportunity and intense competition simultaneously. Add to this the need for corporate transparency and integrity being imposed by consumer pressure and surveillance, and you have a totally new cocktail of pressures to come to terms with.

—— Your customers are about to have a field day. A tale of passion, betrayal, and revenge! ——

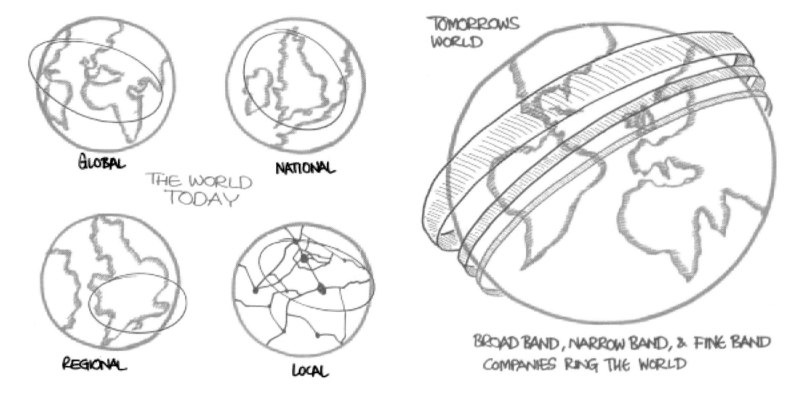

GLOBAL

NATIONAL

THE WORLD TODAY

REGIONAL

LOCAL

TOMORROWS WORLD

BROAD BAND, NARROW BAND, & FINE BAND COMPANIES RING THE WORLD

All companies will be global but not the same width

A tidal wave of choice

A tidal wave of choice is about to sweep away the traditional way of thinking about companies. No longer will global companies sell globally, large companies sell nationally and intracontinentally, medium size sell to regional markets and small companies sell to local markets; all companies will soon seek to operate on a global basis using a web of partners.

The next generation of companies will change from being global down to local, to being broadband, narrow band or fine band. Broadband companies will have a major global presence with a strong brand promise relevant to the range of associated products and services they provide. Narrow band will provide regional flavours on a global basis, relying heavily on global partners including customer guardians to provide local service support. Fine band will provide niche services to specialist interest groups but on a global basis.

Those fine band companies that embrace the customer service ethic, coupled to all the knowledge of an expert in their field and a deep personal interest, will be a hard act to beat.

New fine band global companies will be a hard act to follow

It's a flat world

Many years ago it was proved, completely against popular belief, that the world is round not flat. Maybe, after all these years, we are about to revert to a flat world again.

Consumers and entrepreneurs in developing countries are about to enjoy unprecedented access to western and other developed world markets. Leap-frogging the legacy of technologies slowing down established western companies, and with an abundance of spirited good value labour, companies in the developing world are going to have a fantastic chance to compete in the west. Trading over the net it doesn't matter where you are based as long as you have a spot-on customer ethic and a cool style.

At long last, a level playing field.

It is quite easy to argue, in fact, that not only are we moving to a level playing field, the odds are actually stacked in the favour of developing nations. Not only are there considerable land and labour cost advantages but also the strong reliance on extended families as the core to businesses in some developing countries is perfect for value– and virtue-based working.

The attitude towards service that exists across large parts of Asia and the Far East could also be significant. People often talk about the USA as the home of good service, but I would definitely beg to differ. The USA is OK for high-gloss, mass-produced, 'have a nice day' service linked directly to an almost compulsory tip, but when it comes to natural grace, charm, and a genuine pride in providing immaculate service, forget it.

The best service I have ever experienced has always been in the Far East, where service is a valued profession, and a good door keeper is treated with the same respect as a good chairman. In fact, the very best service I can remember was at a fantastic hotel in Borneo where you really felt that all the staff without exception were genuinely pleased to see you, absolutely nothing was too much trouble, and no one would accept a tip.

That is what I call service. If there are any hotel or restaurant workers reading this, can you put your hand on your heart, and say that the same is true where you work? If not, stop everything you are doing, forget all the trivia, and start to build a service experience that will blow your customers' boots off!

—— **Start building a service experience to blow your customers' boots off!** ——

The reputation race

The balance of power between companies and consumers is, without any doubt, changing. This is not going to be a small issue that you can work around and carry on in largely the same way. Morally bankrupt (or 'rip off the world') thinking is set to be rapidly punished by voracious consumers and competitors. If you don't start thinking about your customers in a completely different light then you're in trouble.

Sunning it

Aside from the flat earth theory, the other popularly held view about the world was that the earth was at the centre of the universe and the sun and other planets revolved around it. This was such a strongly held belief that if you dared to think or say anything to the contrary there was a pretty good chance you were about to meet a long, drawn-out, nasty death as a heretic.

I've got to say that that attitude sums up the way business is conducted today. Companies are the centre of the universe, and consumers revolve around them.

People may have got away with thinking and acting like this so far but not for much longer. This is when we will see the real power of the Internet. At long last, the consumer is about to take their place at the centre of the commercial universe.

And just as it was a tough old battle getting people to accept that the earth span around the sun, so a lot of people are going to fight against the new customer order. There will be pain, suffering and fallout.

They say that the dinosaurs died out when a giant meteor hit the earth and sent up huge clouds of dust and debris. If it happened to the dinosaurs, it can happen to you. Neither size nor technology can protect you; even the mightiest will fall with frightening speed. This is what I was thinking about when I settled on *Brand Storm* as the title of the book. Think of being unprotected in the middle of a tornado or hurricane and you start to imagine how your average brand is going to feel over the next few years.

If you want to survive learn to adapt, and fast!

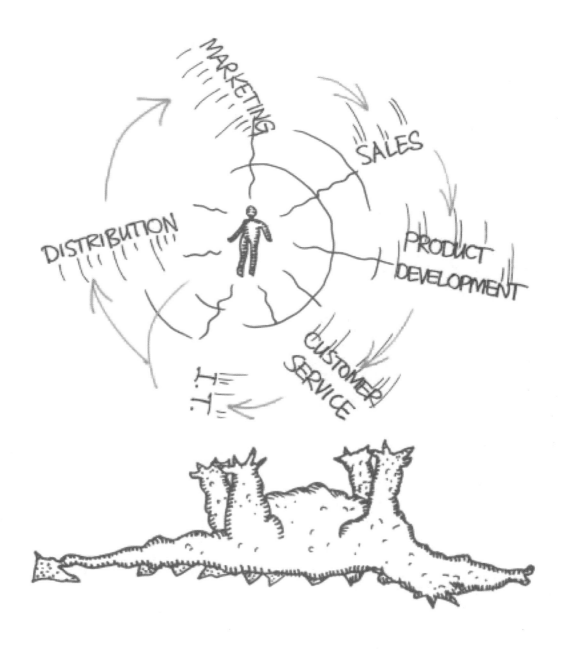

If you're not customer centric then you'll soon be a dead dinosaur

Market cyclones will rip through existing markets blowing away old world companies.

Small and global is now a viable reality.

Infinite choice is becoming a given.

Start believing in your customers.

Get ready to offer serious service value.

Be prepared for customer surveillance.

Strive to make your customers' lives better while you still can.

KICKER:

If you're not customer centric, you'll soon be dead.

Forget all the nonsense about first mover advantage and think customer value

Retail or bust

The high street? What high street?

Having looked at the changes in the relationships between consumers and companies, what impact is all this going to have on the traditional high street?

I guess the easy answer to that question is – dramatic. I must say though that I'm not a first division doom merchant when it comes to the future of the high street not like some people. The changes that have happened over the last 40 years hint at the enormous versatility of the high street, and as Mark Twain once said, news of its death is greatly exaggerated.

To understand fully the future of retail shopping today you need a really clear view not only of shopping but of exactly what the Internet is about and what, if any, threat it poses.

When you talk about the high street to anyone they will probably be able to close their eyes and form a pretty accurate mental picture of your average high street, based on one they actually know. They know how it feels to walk up and down, what it smells like, what they enjoy, and what they hate about it. If you push them a bit harder, they will describe a supermarket, a department store, an out of town shopping centre, and even a retail leisure park. They can do all this because physical retail shopping is an integral part of their lives, and probably has been for as long as they can remember.

If you ask people what they think of the Internet, the average person will start talking e-commerce and how electronic shopping is the future. They are wrong.

At the heart of most of today's Internet hysteria is the biggest lie of the 21st century so far. The Internet is not about e-commerce, it's about customers. Virtually every penny that people are falling over themselves to throw down the drain is being wasted because of this fatal misunderstanding.

Sloppy thinking has always been wrong and is now more wrong than ever. Think about it: if the real impact of the Internet is enfranchised consumers the question to be addressed is not, how can I use the Internet to make money, but how can I use the Internet to delight my customers? It may seem like a small point, but it is the key to understanding the future of both traditional retailing and electronic shopping.

At heart the Internet is still the Information Super Highway, not a great shopping centre in the sky.

Interpull

At the moment there are two key motivations to be on the Internet: greed and fear.

And it's the same whether you are managing a team of people or setting up a new venture, greed and fear are not great motivators. People are currently in the grip of interpull fever. They are being sucked into the Internet for fear of being left out. While I commend people's desire to take action, it doesn't follow that any action is better than no action.

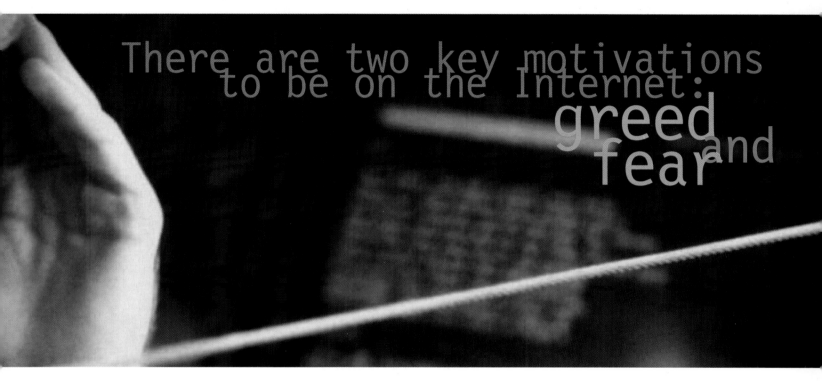

There are two key motivations to be on the Internet: greed and fear

E-tailers see the Internet as a cheap route to market and retailers as either a protection mechanism or a chance to increase convenience for customers who are short of time. This will not be enough. Every successful e-venture must have an e-vantage. And what is that? An e-vantage is a substantive customer benefit greater than being the first in and providing convenience and cheaper prices.

There are countless considerations when creating an e-vantage but they mainly fall into the following categories:

Marketing

Technology

Product

Distribution

Customer service

Overall customer benefit

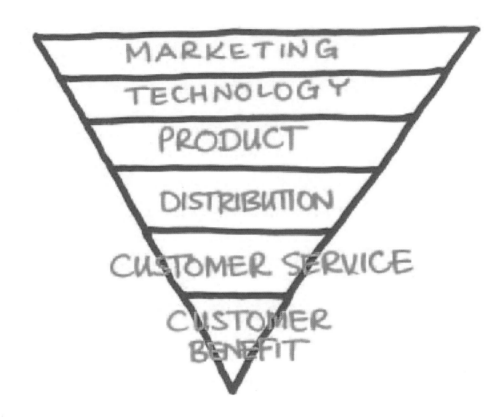

Too much marketing and not enough value

If you look at the time and importance people are attaching to each of these, you start to see why there is a problem. Add to this the fact that new ventures are being rushed to market in a fraction of the time previously taken and you can see why, in some cases, people never even get round to customer benefit before they are actually up and running.

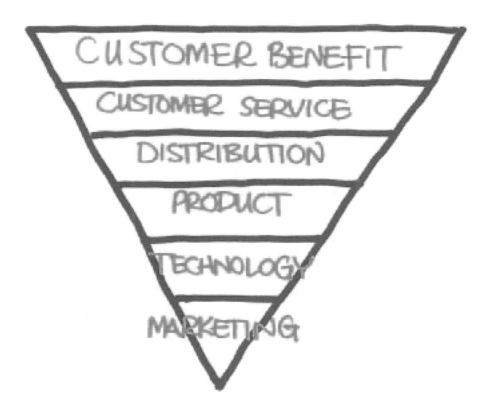

When you think about where the customer e-vantage is created it's easy to see that this needs turning around.

Babies and bath water

So why be a retailer? Why not? Let's not throw the baby out with the bath water. Retailing has done pretty well for the last 2,000 years or so, thank you very much. It is not an issue of to retail or not, it's about scale and relativity. Of course, there will be a thriving traditional retail market, but what shape and form will it be?

Let's look at the basic figures. Mail order has been around five percent of the total retail market for as long as I can remember, and beyond. The balance of companies and products sold has changed, but the total percentage has been remarkably steady.

What impact are the Internet and other new technologies going to have on the volume of remote shopping? Who knows, but if I were a betting man I certainly wouldn't put any money on it more than doubling as a percentage in the next few years and if it reaches 15 percent that would be a major result. Beyond that, I believe that it is currently still in the lap of the gods, and dependent on the strategies and performance of the key retail and e-tail players.

So what does this mean for the high street? To start with, it means change. If you look at the top-line figures, a 15 percent year-on-year drop in sales would probably be about enough to put most retailers out of business, bearing in mind the high degree of fixed and fairly fixed costs.

But not all product areas, and not all retailers, will be hit equally, and not all retailers will have the same opportunity to be able to exploit Internet advantages equally well.

So the short answer to the high street debate is that some high streets and some retailers are going to have a field day and others are going to go to the wall.

What, then, is the key to success or failure on the high street? An r-vantage, that's what.

Get an r-vantage or go bust

PRODUCTION

WHOLESALE

RETAIL

CUSTOMER

So what makes an r-vantage? I'm not going to go into a detailed analysis of the retail market. I will leave that to the professional retailers but there are a couple of points that are worth mentioning with regard to both individual retailers and high streets or other retail destinations.

Changing perspective

The old commercial hierarchy was very product dominated.

RETAIL

SUPPLIERS

CUSTOMERS

Today's economy is retail dominated

In recent years the growth in the scale of retailers, the introduction of EPOS systems, and latterly loyalty cards, have served to change the balance of power. Retailers pushed manufactures away from their customers and began to dominate the food chain.

In the human economy neither of these will do. No longer will individual companies be able to meet the growing expectations of enfranchised consumers. New integrated commercial networks collaborating together are the way forward. Gone will be the old supply chain concept, here comes the customer spin.

Winning spins

With customer spin the boundaries between e-tailing and retailing disappear, to be replaced by a cycle of customer-centric functions. The mix and match ingredients can be spun together to fit any opportunity. When you identify a new customer need, create a new spin designed specifically to exceed your customer grouping's exact expectations.

Making customer spin work will require a degree of self-awareness, humility, and co-operation that is rare in today's corporate environment. But it is the key to corporate success in tomorrow's human economy. No one element should dominate the spin or become sole leader, close working becomes not just important but critical.

So what about the individual elements of the spin in the context of the human economy? Well, each bears a quick examination.

Creating products

This will be very interactive, involving all the spin partners including customers. Mutual risk sharing, to develop new products will become common. Some spin partners will evolve towards share swapping and full partner status in a similar way to the kairetsu principle in Japan. The connecting factors for these companies will be their values and virtues.

Supplying products

Similar to the existing model but with clear channel strategies in place. Manufacturers will sell direct, through web-based and bricks and mortar outlets. Own-brand partnerships between manufacturers and other spin members, sold exclusively by the spin, will become a major new force in the world markets.

Making customer spin work will require a degree of self-awareness and humility rare in today's corporate environment

Lifestyle information

Provision of quality information on all aspects of a customer's lifestyle can only grow in importance. Spin partners will need to mix information about their products, vision, values, and virtues with generally interesting relevant information that customers can use to base their lifestyle decisions on. Highly selective television and magazine-quality media and journalism, centred around the spin partners' values and virtues, will become the backbone of customer communication.

Market awareness

Formerly known as advertising. As you would expect, the role will be similar to the role in the past but the task is now far harder. The proliferation of routes to market and of media channels will make today's mass coverage a thing of the past. Tailoring and planning campaigns will be vital and word of mouth is set to become tomorrow's tv. The role of the new ad agency will be to provide things for customers to talk about. Relationships between creative companies and other members of the spin will become more permanent as sharing values and virtues starts to dominate as a market force.

Customer access

This is what you would know as shops and Internet sites. No longer the all encompassing role it used to be. Retailers and e-tailers will concentrate on creating strong meaningful brands and concepts, while co-operating with suppliers to develop and co-brand unique new products jointly. Customer service, in-store environment, web design, and web mechanics will be core disciplines. Providing world-class customer access will be like running a great magazine. You need to create a powerful editorial feel that customers can strongly relate to, based on fixed values and virtues, but constantly evolving in tone and content.

_____ **Word of mouth is set to become tomorrow's tv** _____

Customer experience

How loved will your customers need to feel? A lot more than they do today! This is the purpose of customer experience.

With unlimited choice of potential suppliers and instant web-based price comparisons, customer experience will be the most important factor in where a customer chooses to shop. The human factor will be the outstanding element of any retail mix, so both web-based and retail traders will concentrate on improving their customer experience as much as possible.

On its own, however, this will not be enough. Whether you are web-based or brick based, with rising customer expectations and rampant competition, even the most ardent traders will need to call on customer guardians.

For many retailers, the provision of an 'at home', personal shopping service for valued customers will become a cost of being in business. For any e-tailer, physical points of presence in remote locations will be a significant part of establishing customer confidence and play an important role in creating awareness.

Customer guardians will concentrate entirely on delighting customers via a range of full-scale, standalone sites, and smaller concessions providing additional customer experience for a number of agreed traders. In addition to dedicated sites, customer guardians will recruit networks of highly trained and well-supported customer experts with the right attitude for delighting demanding customers in their own homes.

Physical distribution

This is a development on the current theme. The emphasis will be on flexibility and hybrid delivery, with a range of delivery options available to support both store and web-based shopping. Flexibility with regard to both time and location will take over from pure speed as the critical success factor. Very local distribution centres, for customer pick-up, and as a hub for home delivery, could eventually be the norm.

———— The provision of an 'at home' personal shopping service will become a cost of ————
being in business

Customer guardians

Losing customers is an unforgivable sin today. Tomorrow, in the human economy, it will be punishable by death. A high attrition rate, with its associated customer gossip quota, will kill you. It is that simple.

Some people think that customers will always flow into their business, like water out of a spring well. Sorry, but not any more. Even for businesses with a traditionally transitory audience, such as tourist sites, fairs, and around sporting venues, customers will disappear faster than an endangered species. The reason being the enfranchised consumer. Community websites will review performance, even of mobile fairs and the like. Poor-quality or rogue traders will be sitting ducks.

At the higher end of the market, the same issues apply but expectations will be higher. Customers with unsolved complaints will torment formerly impregnable companies.

The real problem in all this is that if a company is not created entirely around a service ethic, however hard you try reversing it, delivering world-beating service will always be a problem. And in a world with few other means of differentiation, that is a real problem.

The answer, at least in part, is to use professionals. Stop customer service and complaint handling being a rather unfashionable and problematic part of the company and make it the sole responsibility of a customer guardian set up to do nothing but placate and then delight your customers.

The relationship you establish with your customer guardian, like all the relationships in a customer spin, is critical. It should not be like the easy come easy go, cost-driven relationships that have sprung up between companies and their call centres. The service some customers are receiving from agency call centres is nothing short of dire at one extreme, and adequate and impersonal at the other. In these organisations, customers are transactions which just will not work in the human economy.

Your customer guardian must totally understand and share your values and virtues. He/she should be a partner in the full sense of the word, sharing more than just a financial interest in your business. Fees should be based on customer perception measures, not purely on a transactional basis. It is also critical that they are given total responsibility to settle any issue on your behalf, almost like an independent arbiter.

—— **Losing customers is an unforgivable sin today. Tomorrow it will be punishable by death** ——

Get Physical

If the shape and form of retailers is set dramatically to change, what is the future of the actual high street and other retail locations?

Clearly, the Internet phenomenon is going to be kinder to some retail operations and locations than others.

Having said that, the key to success will again be the ability to adapt. I am convinced that there need not be a death warrant over any retail site; the problems that occur will be of the retailer's own making.

Major retail sites, such as standalone supermarkets, out of town department stores and major new purpose built shopping centres, should be in complete control of their own destiny. They need to set up effective customer spins, perfect their service and create environments that are a joy to behold. They also need to blur the edges between retailing, e-tailing and entertainment, but none of that should be beyond them. If they fail, it will be because they haven't taken the opportunities open to them, taken their customers seriously, or treated them with proper respect.

At the other end of the spectrum, pretty small high streets are in a strong position. Again they have to take their service by the scruff of the neck, and start to treat their customers with respect, but they can if they want to. They need to ensure that the whole high street is a pleasure to visit, turn it into a highly individual, convenient, leisure destination. They should have done all that already. They need individuality, quality, peace, and tranquillity together with sufficient themed variety to amuse a whole family, leaving them begging for more. Oh, and don't rip off the customers with ludicrous prices.

If many retailers fail it is because they deserve to

Time to kick butt

But what about the poor guys in the middle? Dull suburban high streets, many as ugly as sin, every other shop a charity shop, peeling paint, and rubbish all over the place. Not a pretty sight, and competition from everywhere.

What a fantastic opportunity!

What is required is a totally radical rethink, with tones of imagination, and amazing co-operation between councils, property companies, and the retailers themselves. OK, I know I'm asking a lot, but boy, will it be worth it.

Many of these high streets are surrounded by reasonably affluent areas, and even if they are not, what a fantastic chance to create an oasis of new age, urban chic on the cheap, and make a fortune doing it.

Don't think about these areas as they currently are, concentrate on the basic raw materials and potential. Relatively wide roads, most with rear access, and some dedicated parking. Interesting, in a quasi-industrial, commercial, loft type of way, buildings that may be a bit ugly now but with the designer treatment and the right marketing can be the next Chelsea Harbour.

Review the mix of property use. These high streets are already dying on their feet just from the effect of out of town shopping let alone the Internet. Now is the time to start thinking about them as multitasking brown field sites, ready for a new life. City dwelling is already funky, now is the time to change high street dwelling from bedsit of last resort over a fast food shop to the ultimate in lifestyle living.

You need a cunning plan and this is where the co-operation from property companies and the council is needed. Plan a new mix of retail shops, restaurants, wine bars, and fun modern residential accommodation and yesterday's 1950's depression is new millennium revival, complete with on-site punters hot to offload their cash.

What a fantastic chance to create an oasis of new age, urban chic on the
cheap, and make a fortune doing it

Good riddance

Good riddance to all those boring old estate agents, banks, and other so-called service shops that are busily closing all their branches to save cash as fast as they can. You can't say they ever did much to enhance the neighbourhood, can you? The Internet is the best place for them.

I guess what I am trying to illustrate is not that there is this one great solution to all high streets, but that the possibilities are endless for those that work with imagination.

And work is required. It needs to be radical and it needs to start happening now. We are entering a radical time. Medium size high streets that do nothing are in severe danger and their further demise would be a great loss to everyone. You are limited only by your imagination.

— If you have any connection with a local high street, don't be ordinary, be extraordinary

SNAPSHOT

The future of the high street is totally up for grabs, with fortune favouring the brave.

Sloppy e-thinking and unfounded hope will cost you millions.

Don't think e-tail or retail, think both.

Supply cycle co-operation and customer spins are the only future.

In-home personal shopping will become a cost of sale.

High Street hybrids herald a new suburban age.

However you trade, you need a clear customer advantage beyond price and convenience.

KICKER:

Trash the retail rulebook and e-business essentials.

Customer love

I'm free!

5

With the human economy revolving around consumers, what will they be thinking and doing?

It is a fair bet that, to start, with they will be in a state of shock. Freedom, for those who have never experienced, it is a rich dish to digest. If you are stuck in an institution where you are told what to think, what is right, and what is wrong, you get to the point where you rely on being told what to do. It will take some time for consumers to realise that they have taken over the asylum.

There will also be a lag as Internet literacy catches up with technology and Internet fear is striped away bit by bit, till using the Internet is as easy as using the tv.

For most people their first experience of the Internet is right up there with their other firsts, such as their first drink of alcohol or first drive a car. Trying the Internet for the first time gives you an amazing buzz linked to a wonderful sense of freedom. It really is quite a rush. All you want to do is explore this endless world of information, trying every experience it has to offer.

But the buzz doesn't last, and eventually you slow down and start to ask, 'What can the internet actually do for me?' Society as a whole will follow a similar path: first it will enjoy the media-fuelled excitement; then it will explore the possibilities that are presented to it; after that it will stop and think there must be more to this than we are getting so far.

At this point both consumers, as individuals, and society as a whole, will take control of their lives, and grab the opportunities the Internet provides. Life trends will emerge around consumers with different Internet attitudes. Some people will actively embrace Internet power, and become consumer champions, while others will take a more laid-back approach.

—— **With the human economy revolving around consumers, what will they be thinking and doing** ——

Virtual unreality

One of the greatest determinants of future life will be the degree to which individuals are prepared to enter the virtual world of cyberspace. Will a person need interaction with other people, or will all their needs be satisfied virtually?

Using emerging technological advances as a guide it is easy to conclude that we will never need each other again. Add to this the way some people have already embraced the web socially, and you will be convinced of it. E-life is clearly going to be a reality for some people, but just how universal will it become, and what will it mean on a day-to-day basis?

How isolated is that?

What does isolation mean to you? Is it solitary confinement, and working alone in a lighthouse, or is it sitting at home chatting to people on the Internet who you have never physically met? Are you happy for your relationships with family, friends, and even lovers to become virtual? One man's isolation is rapidly becoming another man's night out with friends.

It will take some time for consumers to realise that they have taken over the asylum

One man's isolation is rapidly becoming another man's night out with friends

Let's look at some facts:

People are spending more time online and when they do they spend less time with friends and family and go out less.

People don't know their neighbours as well as they used to.

Voyeurism and social detachment are on the increase.

People socialise less in the area where they live.

Parks and local amenities are deteriorating and local shops closing as a result.

Overall, people are talking less.

Working hours are generally longer.

Remote working and hot-desking are on the up.

E-mail is reducing phone and personal contact.

We are being deluged by infotainment.

Lies, damned lies and statistics

If you accept the facts and the emerging trends then we are all going one way. But I don't see it. At the moment the Internet is sexy and people are experimenting. The novelty value is greater than the experience, and for a time this doesn't matter.

But ultimately the Internet is about choice, the choice to opt in and to opt out. Just because you *can* do something doesn't mean you *have* to. Human nature is not going to change, and at heart most people, though not all, still prefer the company of people to talking to a machine.

This is what will separate the full-blown human economy from the transitional phase we are going through now. Empowered, self confident consumers will see through the hype and demand to be treated how they want, when they want.

Gut reactions

So how exactly are consumers likely to behave?

Consumers will crystallise into three distinct types (dependent, free and liberated) based on a whole cocktail of personal experiences and prejudices.

Most consumers will have an underlying predisposition to one of these categories: they will be intrinsically dependent, free or liberated by nature.

Every consumer will, however, exhibit signs of all three categories to varying degrees when faced with various propositions. Some buying decisions will be of greater significance to that individual's psyche while other decisions will relate to a separate part of that person's life. A decision made on behalf of a child may be made differently to one made on one's own behalf.

The significance of these customer types will become clear when we consider how companies should deal differently with each type.

Habit is dependence forming

Dependent customers

Dependent customers are the bedrock of commerce – reliable and steadfast when treated well. Their dependence can be based on a number of different factors.

Tradition and pure comfort will be a strong pull. In an age of constant change comfort will be gained from constancy. The human desire for nesting will, in part, be met by surrounding oneself with familiar products in an increasingly unfamiliar, and, at times, frightening world. Using the same washing up liquid as your parents used will connect you to your past.

Geography will remain a factor for dependent customers. If the product or service is not a vital part of a person's life, the 'closest is easiest' rule will still count. People still have a preference for the local if there is no strong reason to want otherwise.

Cost will be a major factor for dependent customers. If a product is superb value and does what you need it to, you may well go onto auto pilot and use your scarce thinking time to make more important decisions. Those that are short of time and cash are particularly likely to become dependent users if the people they are buying from respect their custom and don't abuse their status as supplier of choice.

Convenience will be another powerful inducement to dependence. If you make a person's life easy and you are consistent in what you do, people will come to depend on you as they develop other aspects of their lives. Reliability will be all if you want to maintain this dependence. Habit builds dependence. If you make your product a distinctive part of an individual's personal ritual there is a strong chance that dependence will become established on your product or service.

At the other end of the spectrum, fashion, aspiration, and the need to belong to something will also induce dependence. If your product has strong aspirational virtues, endorsements and connotations then these will deliver loyalty; the need to belong to some form of club associated with certain brands will be a dominant factor. The only downside here is that the explosion of popular media and culture will churn out pure fashion brands at a rate of knots. If you want longevity for your brand, even as a fashion statement, it will need depth and integrity.

There is a strong correlation between dependent customers and the purchase of physical products. The emphasis for both retailers and manufacturers selling to dependent customers will be consistency, reliability, and distinctiveness.

Free customers

Free customers are a different kettle of fish. These guys are hot. Perpetually seeking innovation and pushing back the boundaries, they enjoy technical freedom and are always at the leading edge of new technology.

Looking for an adrenaline rush, they want to be amused. They enjoy a greater degree of commercial freedom than other customers do, and are very lifestyle or business style focused. Always up for the latest experience, they are good spenders but enjoy being commercially promiscuous.

Free customers are more service focused than product focused; living life has more appeal than the outright acquisition of material goods. Young at heart, if not always in years, the free customer is a sensation seeker. If you want to party, get in with the free set; they may not change the world, but, boy, do they make it more fun.

Any organisation looking to delight a free customer must be focused on new experiences, funky, and hot to trot.

Free customers enjoy being commercially promiscuous

Liberated customers value **trust** *and* meaning

Liberated customers

Where the free guys are hot these dudes are cool.

Usually well networked and well informed they are self-actuated and mature. Movers and shakers, these are the people that will either change the way the world works or just make it a better place by being part of it.

Liberated customers value trust and meaning. They are relationship orientated, both personally and commercially. They are looking for more than surface attraction and have an enormous capacity to be loyal.

They believe in enhancement and empowerment both in their own lives and for those they deal with. Liberated customers are more focused on relationships than products or services. They appreciate the human touch, and will see through the merely ephemeral and kitsch.

Companies that want to transact with liberated customers need to be there for the long term and treat their customers with respect and reverence.

Convolve and Grow

If understanding and relating with your customers is going off the scale in importance, how do you know your customers properly, learn to exceed their expectations, and still make some money?

The answer is a degree of customer involvement as yet unseen, become a convolved (customer involved) company. With consumer surveillance, keeping your customers at arm's length is no longer an option, so go the other way, throw open your doors and invite your customers in.

Consumers are better informed than ever. With the Internet in full swing, anything you know, so do they. You no longer need to be a research professional to see inside consumers' heads, and, as they say at the Fourth Room, you can't research the future.

Up close and personal is better than uptight and distant

Go out into your customers' lives, persuade a few customer families to let one of your directors live with them for a week. Up-close and personal is better than uptight and distant. If your customers are gracious enough to buy from you, they must surely be worth the effort in return. Reward them well for their trouble, remembering the power of word of mouth and the consumer jungle drums.

Start recruiting non-executive consumers to your board, let your customers see how you run the company. Introduce your customers to your suppliers and partners.

If these are such hard thoughts to consider, are you running your company the right way for the human economy? Now is the time to weave a consumer thread into the very fabric of your organisation. Use a shared language, live a shared life, think about how to reward each other.

What about making money?

The human economy won't change the need for a positive bottom line, much to the chagrin of a host of Internet companies. With people wanting more of what they want per pound or dollar they spend, is there an answer?

Luckily, yes.

- Decide who you want your customers to be and stick with them.

- Immerse yourself in your customers' lives.

- Learn about what they value.

- Empathise with them.

- Focus.

- Be clear about what your customers will pay for.

- Be the world's best at providing it.

- Cut out anything else.

- Don't be distracted by your own agenda.

- Constantly check how you are doing.

- Don't over-engineer your service.

Love hurts

We are entering a war zone, a customer service war zone, where commercial success will depend on providing appropriate but viable customer service. Doing the right things is fine but they all cost money. How much can you afford to spend? The answer lies in identifying the type of customer buying your products, and not over-engineering your service.

don't over engineer
your service

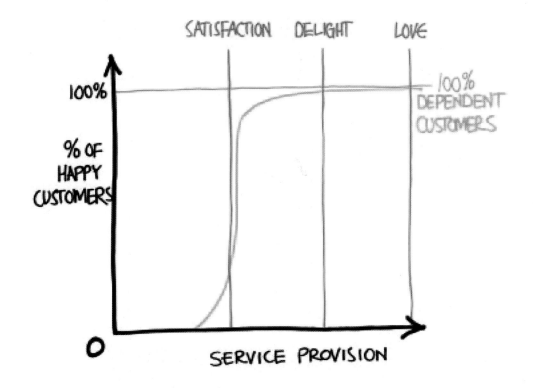

If your customers are dependent, satisfy them

Set your service at a level to satisfy your customers' expectations.

Why waste money you can't afford? Use it where it is needed. Produce a fit for purpose product with world-class performance and promotion, obvious distinction, and unbeatable prices for what you offer. It's not about cheap, it's about value. No one can undercut you for a long time if you are not wasting a penny.

Be proud of what you do, and do it well.

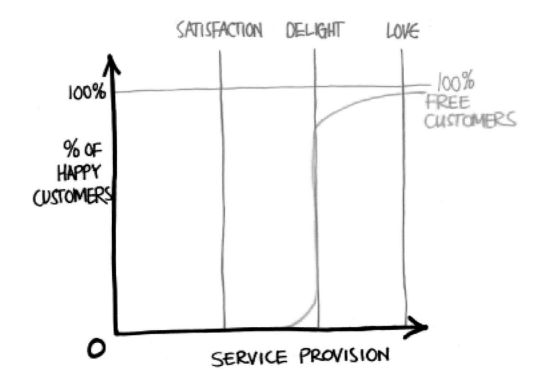

If your customers are free, delight them

Set your service levels to delight your customers.

Customer delight will cost you more, but free customers expect more from their supplier. Virtual service isn't easy to deliver well. Let your customers down once and they will never forgive you. High delight retailing is not easy to deliver well, either. It's not just the shopping that counts, it's the entertainment.

These guys want excitement, so give it to them. They expect to be delighted every time, but, whatever you do, remember, you're only as good as your latest trick. It doesn't matter how much you give them; they aren't into long-term relationships. When a new face hits town they'll be off. This is a volume game. Keep those new customers coming, and keep the old ones sweet enough not to slag you off to their friends.

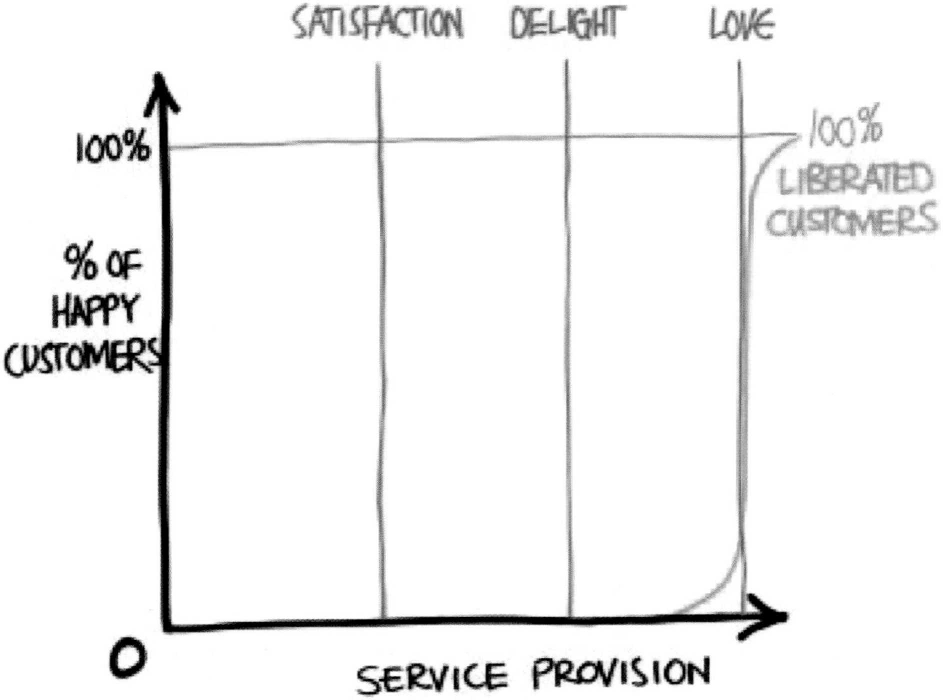
SATISFACTION
DELIGHT
LOVE
100%
% OF HAPPY CUSTOMERS
100% LIBERATED CUSTOMERS
0
SERVICE PROVISION

If your customers are liberated, love them

Set your service levels to make your customers feel loved.

These customers are worth their weight in gold. Look after them, and they will look after you. Technology is a given here, what will make the difference are human values such as respect. Fail to treat liberated customers as individuals, and they will be lost to you, leaving you hurt and lonely.

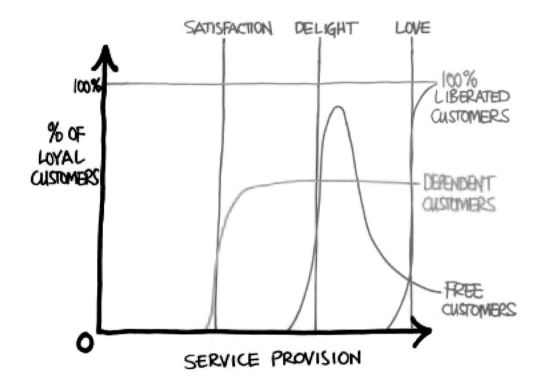

The loyalty equation

In the human economy, understanding the loyalty equation is the key to sustainable profit. If it were purely better service the solution would be relatively easy, but it is not. Oppressive competition will not allow you to spend a penny you don't need to.

The answer is to understand the relationship between customer experience and loyalty for each type of customer. With the cost of acquiring new customers spiraling ever up, it is loyalty you need to spend your money on, not solely making your customers happy. Your customers are still loyal, but maybe not to you.

Your customers are still loyal, but maybe not to you

Crack your loyalty conundrum and strike it rich

- Consistent service and good value are the key to dependent customers. Deliver more and you waste your money; let them down and they won't come back.

- Concentrate on finding a never ending stream of new experiences and new delights for your free customers rather than trying to delight them more.

- Deliver the very best for your liberated customers, and they will pay you back for years, but only the very best, most personalised service will create the loyalty you need.

SNAPSHOT

As we enter a virtual world, knowing how your customers expect to be treated will be everything.

Do your customers depend on you?

Are your customers commercially promiscuous?

Are your customers into trust and meaning?

Can you satisfy your customers?

Are you delighting your customers?

Do your customers love you?

You're customers are probably still loyal, but are they loyal to you?

KICKER:

Learn how to value your customers' loyalty if you want to strike it rich.

Corporate karma

KARMA – car'ma

1 **The total effect of a person's actions and conduct during the successive phases of the person's existence, regarded as determining the person's destiny.**

2 **The doctrine of fate as the result of cause and effect, the theory of inevitable consequence.**

3 **The aura, atmosphere or feeling surrounding something.**

Although these descriptions are of karma in the traditional sense, as related to individuals, it doesn't take a huge leap of the imagination to apply the word to organisations and companies.

Corporate karma is the perfect destination for brand storm. Everything discussed so far revolves around the need for self-knowledge, integrity, and an understanding of your customers in an environment where the fraudulent or sloppy will be rapidly found out.

The purpose of this part of *Brand Storm* is to unify all the strands in the book together to help you create brands with integrity and companies with assured purpose. The concept of cause and effect and the theory of inevitable consequence are highly applicable in the human economy and reiterate the fact that your development over the next few years is entirely in your own hands.

Cheat your customers and bad karma goes with you

Brand evolution

I guess at this stage in the book it useful to address, however briefly, the whole issue of what a brand is.

A great deal of time and energy has been spent on this over the years, defining exactly what a brand is, and how it compares to other terms such as identity and reputation. People will no doubt argue forever, but one thing is clear, brands before them, and commodities have evolved considerably over time.

To start with there were commodities: gold was gold, iron was iron.

Then came the first brands, and they were literally that, hot iron meeting flesh, declaring ownership of, say, sheep or cows.

Hot on the heals of ownership brands came quality and quantity brands such as hallmarks.

With the advent of mass production came brand identifiers such as Levi's and Cadbury's. Image marketing was born using advertising as a vehicle.

The next developments were icon brands summing up a whole mood such as Benneton or Nike, and corporate brands using badge engineering to unite monoliths like Microsoft and IBM.

The ultimate stage is brand as elixir of life, the spark from which a new life grows, and the unique DNA that shapes the development of every aspect of an organisation is formed. This is what I mean when I use the word 'brand'.

To me 'brand' means everything connected to the essence of a company. The directors, all the people, the products, the company itself, its logo, its physical visual presence, its voice, its reputation, its associations and endorsements, its customer perception, and the sum total of the company's communication. It means every incarnation, and every living, breathing second of an organisation's life.

Brand is the elixir of life, the spark from which all life grows

No more heroes

In the human economy, the massive increase in the number of virtual and real channels to market, together with the growth of individual market offers, will make the universal marketing that companies pursue today increasingly difficult to achieve. In fact, the human economy will sound the death knell of the superman brand.

Using the holistic brand definition I've just described, I want to look at the type of brands that will develop to provide the various customer service levels discussed earlier: customer satisfaction, customer delight, and customer love.

Using customer service as a basis, you can divide brands into three categories: performance brands delivering customer satisfaction to dependent customers, personality brands delivering customer delight to free customers; and partner brands generating love from liberated customers.

Each one of these three brand categories will focus its marketing effort differently to meet the needs of its type of customers profitably. But how are they going to ensure that they achieve the right type of marketing focus?

Let me introduce the new *Brand Storm* marketing mix. Gone are the four P's of yesteryear, in come the four C's for performance brands, the four D's for personality brands, and the new four P's for partner brands.

C	D	P
Character	Difference	People
Capability	Delivery	Partnership
Care	Delight	Promise
Cost	Dynamics	Professionalism

The human economy will sound the death knell of the superman brand

Performance brands

These are the bedrock of the commercial world, and will deliver customer satisfaction to dependent customers via the four C's.

Performance brands will be rooted in features and benefits, both real and perceived. At one end of the spectrum, they may be functional, practical or useful while at the other, they may be aspiration, prestige, and association driven.

Performance brands will often be associated with physical products but there are no hard and fast rules except that performance brands must always do what is expected of them as a minimum.

Betray your customers and feel their revenge

The primary marketing focus of performance brands will be around the four Cs:

Character

This is the innate character and image of your product or service. Many of the traditional promotional aspects of brand development will be important here: advertising, promotion, packaging, endorsements, associations, etc.

Capability

This is the performance of your product or service. How good is it at doing what you say it will? How reliable is it? The critical factor in capability is not only comparison to competition but performance against the expectation you have created with your customer. Honesty is vital.

Care

Care relates to all aspects of your customer service experience: your guarantees, your help desks, your in-store service and your sales experience. Courtesy and efficiency are the base line. Don't let this slip. Betray your customers, and you will feel their revenge.

Cost

In the human economy, with price transparency, cost will always be important to performance brands. Again, it is worth stressing that we are not talking cheap, we are talking fantastic value. Anyone managing a performance brand must ensure that his or her customer's view of value is, first, as broad as possible but, second, correlates to theirs.

We are not talking cheap, we are talking fantastic value

Personality brands

Personality brands will always be at the leading edge of whatever is happening, delighting their customers through novelty and innovation. Most fashion brands will be personality brands. Exploration, excitement, and a constant churn of experience will feature prominently along with immediate satisfaction.

Exploitation of short-term technological advantage will dominate the way personality brands present and deliver their propositions. As you might expect, many solely or substantially Internet-based companies will also be personality brands highlighting the task facing these companies.

Constant exposure to their target audience will be needed to generate awareness and excitement, which, although expensive, is more likely to generate short-term sales leads than any lasting loyalty. Today's several million hits to your Internet site are tomorrow's old news, as many Internet sites are finding out. It is very hard to make an Internet site emotionally engaging.

Personality brands must be like bungee jumping for consumers

The primary marketing focus of personality brands will be around the four D's:

Difference

A powerfully communicated difference is at the heart of personality brands. If you are not perceived as genuinely different, forget it.

Delivery

With a large number of virtual companies being personality brands, end-to-end delivery will be crucial. If an Internet or home delivery company lets a consumer down, they rarely use that company again, and can be vocal in their opinions.

Delight

Overt delight is all for personality brands. Living on the edge with their customers, personality brands must be like bungee jumping for consumers. Live and let rip.

Dynamics

Change, change, and yet more change. As a personality brand, constant evolution around a common purpose is your only role in life. Time to market for new ideas will be a dominant issue with new product and service development their lifeblood. The greater the degree of consumer involvement, the better.

Partner brands

Partner brands are the top of the customer service food chain, designed to enter a love affair with their customers. As is the case with all romantic attachments, it is better for partner brands when their love is not unrequited. Only ultimate service is acceptable for partner brands, but the loyalty they generate justifies it.

Partner brands should be soul mates, they must generate total confidence and trust. Mutual respect and reliability are bywords of partner brands. They must always act responsibly, taking into account the interests of all their stakeholders, including investors, staff, customers, the environment, and society in general.

Partner brands need a robust commercial infrastructure, and strong visible values and virtues. There is a strong possibility that the highest echelons of partner brands will start to fill the vacuum being left by governments and religious organisations.

Partner brands stand up, and are counted

In a marketing sense the priority for partner brands will be the new four P's:

People

People underwrite everything a partner brand stands for, be they customers, staff, or the general public. Values and virtues are even more important to these companies than vision. These companies stand up, and are counted.

Partnership

Almost as important as people is the principle of partnership. This is enshrined in the partner brand constitution as the relationship of choice with everyone.

Promise

A gentleman's word is his bond and so is it with partner brands. Partner brands must never break a promise.

Professionalism

It almost goes without saying: if something is worth doing, partner brands do it well.

Keeping karma

The picture is now building. I have painted a scenario of emerging customer types: dependent, free, or liberated.

I have shown how the appropriate economic responses vary between satisfaction, delight, and love based on the loyalty pattern of each type of customer.

I have created new brand definitions (performance, personality, and partner brands), each one designed to deliver satisfaction, delight or love.

Different brand types need different marketing focus, hence I have introduced the new brand storm marketing mix. Out with the old four P's in with the four C's, D's and new P's.

But is this the whole picture? Is the panorama complete?

Not quite. If we go back to the dictionary definitions of karma and then think about the evolution of brands, the final vista in the panorama will come into focus.

'Karma' was defined as destiny, the inevitable consequence of all actions and conduct. The ultimate stage in the evolution of brands defined as the elixir of life and corporate DNA. Put these together and the only logical conclusion is that there must be a direct correlation between brand types and organisational type. The final stage of brand storm makes those connections and illuminates these new organisational types.

There must be a direct correlation between brand types and organisational type

Be your brands

To maintain public, employee, and commercial confidence, different types of company will evolve to deliver different types of brands. These will not be absolutes but companies will need to be clear about their primary focus, and the balance of the other factors, and reflect this in all their actions.

So what will these organisations be like?

Benefit firsts

The first type is benefit firsts, which will deliver performance brands. These organisations will be rooted in the customer experience of the services and products they deliver. All their brands must have the same robust honesty to them if they want to inspire confidence from their customers; inconsistency will be jumped upon. Not the most obviously sexy type of company, their uniqueness will be constant quality in a shifting world.

Virtual friends

Next come virtual friends, which will deliver personality brands. All the aspects of a personality brand should live in a virtual friend, with innovation and novelty as key aspects. The strength of virtual friends will be in their continual evolution and freshness. They must, however, be clear about their unique purpose, and use it to direct all their various incarnations.

People companies

The last type, people companies, will deliver partner brands. As you would expect, human values must be paramount to a company delivering partner brands. If you want to make your customers feel loved, you must start by making your own team feel loved and involved. People companies will have gravitas, and a sense of responsibility, upon which their customers will rely.

Lack of clarity in any company will be commercial suicide. Decide who you want your customers to be and orientate everything you do around that.

Lack of clarity in any company will be suicide

Top down — bottom up

That, then, is the whole picture, customer to company and back again. So where do you start if you want to bring your company together to achieve your corporate karma?

To my mind it doesn't really matter where you start. It is where you end up that counts. If you have the luxury of a start-up situation, I suggest you start at one end or the other and work forward or back.

———————— It's not where you start. It is where you end up that counts ————————

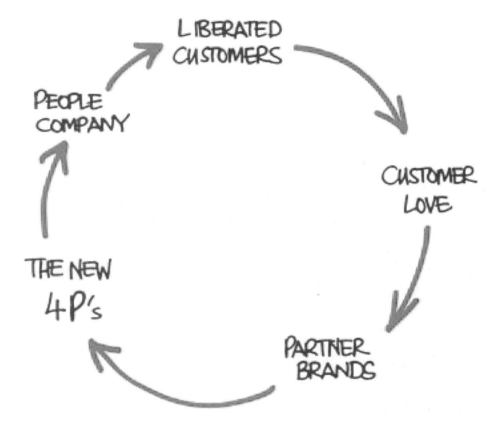

Virtuous circles

If you are dealing with an existing business, break into the cycle wherever you like and work your way round the circle.

The role of brands has evolved; brands are now company DNA, the spark from which all corporate life grows.

The superman brand is dead.

Can your brand perform, and do you care?

Do you have a personality with a difference?

Are you the ideal partner, and do you keep your promises?

Are you the personification of your brand?

If you cheat your customers, bad karma will go with you.

KICKER:

Your destiny is the inevitable consequence of everything you do and everything you say.

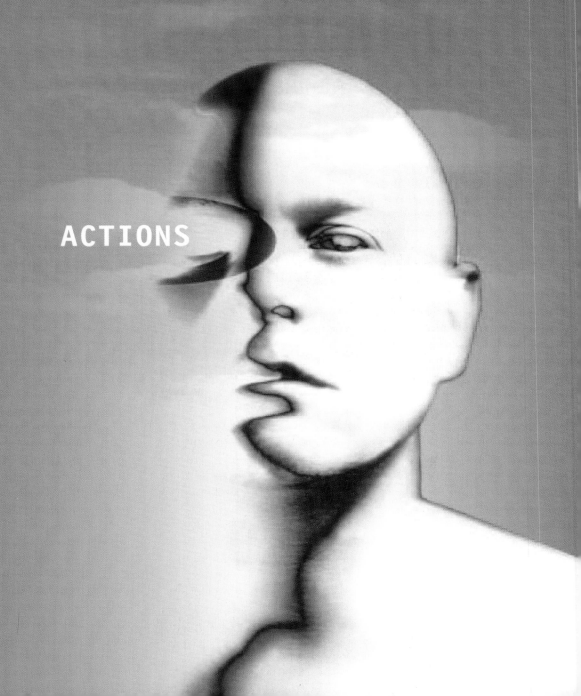

Scene two

ACTIONS

DOING IT

The purpose of Scene One was not to dispense pearls of wisdom, but to help you think about your own unique issues and opportunities.

If you are now thinking about making your customers love you, unifying your brand, and corporate behaviour, cutting out something that fails to inspire you 100 percent or being totally radical, then Scene One has been a success.

But as I have experienced myself on several occasions, being inspired, even being inspired and right, is of no advantage unless you are able to act on your inspiration.

The purpose of Scene Two, then, is simple, to do just that: to help you take action.

The models I use in Scene Two are not overly scientific, in fact, if the basic approach seems familiar, it may well be.

If you have ever completed a simple questionnaire while browsing through a magazine you will recognise the format. Have you found your perfect partner or are you a great lover? I particularly remember one in *Cosmopolitan*, entitled 'Are You A Giver Or A Grabber?' Well, the models in Scene Two are based on this type of quick quiz.

Although I understand that this is not always the case, when it comes to brand storm, size doesn't matter. It will make no difference whether you are part of a huge multinational, a small family firm, or a business start-up. Apply the spirit of brand storm and it will help you forge through any stormy weather, and rocky waters ahead.

Size doesn't matter

Question time

Scene Two focuses on the critical issues for any company in the human economy. Here are several questions which, if you haven't already asked yourself, you need to start asking now!

- Are you the very best at what you do?

- Are there things more important to you than money?

- Is your company's integrity unquestionable?

- Does every aspect of your operation reflect that integrity?

- Do your people and products walk the same talk?

- Are you prepared for the greatest upheaval the branded world has ever experienced?

- How fit is your brand?

- If you cut your company in half does it read 'customer'?

- With an increasing number of people who don't actually work for you involved in helping satisfy your customers, how many have even the faintest idea about your company values and virtues? Or, for that matter, care?

- Do you know for sure whether your staff are loyal to you, each other or just themselves?

- What three things that are designed specifically to foster staff loyalty happen every working day?

- Do you demonstrably live the values you want your team to live?

- How do the best potential recruits feel about your values?

if you cut your company in half does it read 'customer'?

Wishbones

When people want to reassess an existing business or develop an idea for a new business, they often create a series of statements that frame their ambition for their venture. Sometimes these are called vision statements but this doesn't capture the breadth, spirit or, indeed, limitations of what these should be.

What you really need if you want to launch a great company is a great wishbone. So what exactly is a wishbone?

A wishbone is a blueprint for the success of your idea in plain English. It should be the elixir of life for your venture, containing all the unique DNA needed for your future success.

Your wishbone should be the skeleton of your embryonic idea, known, and shared by all involved. It is not a complicated irrelevance, used to fill out your business case, and never sees the light of day again.

Why call it a wishbone? At the stage you write it, that is all it is. To turn a wishbone into a backbone you have to action it.

The structure of the wishbone is not unique; headings have been drafted in from several models including the one used at the Fourth Room. Indeed, neither is it perfect. To my mind, however, it covers the main areas any team will need to agree on if they are going to move forward together as one group.

If you already have a vision statement you will have the start of your wishbone, but my advice is to take this opportunity to review the core purpose of your organisation from scratch.

to turn a wishbone into a backbone, you have to action it

So what does each element mean?

Vision
This is not just your vision for yourself but your vision for the world in which you wish to operate.

BHAG (big hairy audacious goal)
Something huge to strive for collectively and that, if you are honest, brave and believe enough, you can achieve.

Purpose
The unique reason why you are in business.

Promise
Your customer promise.

Approach
Sets the tone for your strategy.

Strategy

How to succeed in your purpose.

Tactics

How you intend to deliver your strategy.

Values

The framework for team behaviour.

Virtues

Laying the foundation of your customers' experience.

Visuals

Set the tone for your visual expression.

Voice

The way you want people to hear you.

The individual elements of the wishbone are not all sequential, or of equal importance, and some will need revision before others. How you implement them will however start to determine whether you stand or fall. To illustrate how a wishbone should look, let's look again at the brand storm wishbone.

The Brand Storm wishbone

Vision

Business success, in the new human economy, through mutual trust.

BHAG (big hairy audacious goal)

To be the first truly, emotionally engaging, enjoyable, and accessible business book.

Purpose

To help you establish economically viable and sustainable trust with your customers, regardless of how you trade with them.

Promise

To enhance your future business prospects in an enjoyable and memorable way.

Approach

To illuminate the future, not just describe it.

To make the ideas actionable, not just fascinating.

To inspire you to want to live your own dreams.

Strategy

To ignite you to take positive action by appealing to your emotions as well as your reason.

To help you implement *Brand Storm* through the brand storm website.

To encourage dialogue between you and the author, and between you and other readers, to create an ongoing and shared experience.

tactics make it fun
make it simple
make it visual
make it dynamic
make it doable

Brand Storm values

→ Openness

→ Fairness

→ Passion

→ Belief

→ Humanity

→ Hope

Brand Storm virtues

→ Insight

→ Imagination

→ Illumination

→ Inspiration

→ Ignition

→ Involvement

Brand Storm visuals

→ Use colour strongly

→ Use space wisely

→ Use simplicity

→ Use emphasis powerfully

→ Illustrate often

Brand Storm voice

→ Open

→ Irreverent

→ Parabolic

→ Joyous

Make a wish

Now is the time to create your own wishbone. Involve as many people as you can, both from within your organisation and from your friends, suppliers, partners, and even customers.

Link up to: www.BrandStorm.com to discuss your progress.

Once you have your wishbone, you can start turning it into the backbone of your organisation, and that is where the other parts of 'Actions' come in. No wishbone will ever be entirely finished. It should continually evolve with use. As your organisation grows so should your wishbone. The next four stages of 'Actions' will help that growing process; they will help both in making your wishbone a reality and also in developing and growing your wishbone into its next evolutionary stage.

When growing your business, there are two important things to remember:

Creating your wishbone and carrying out psyche, spirit, life, and force should always be an iterative process.

If you want people to support your ideas involve them early. Communicate, communicate, communicate.

So what do the next parts of 'Actions' do?

Psyche,
Spirit, Force,
Life

Setting the scene

Take One puts flesh on your wishbone.

'Psyche' helps you develop the central character of your company. Only organisations that learn to harmonise their corporate behaviour with their individual brands will retain the trust of a new generation of aggressively inquisitive customers and customer clubs.

Take Two keeps your wishbone customer and brand focused.

'Spirit' looks at two things, the power of your brand spirit (the strength of your brand in the market place) and your customer spirit or customer focus. Both of these will be put under enormous pressure in the face of exploding supply fuelled by globally empowered Internet companies.

Take Three makes your wishbone real for your people.

'Life' makes values and virtues liveable by bridging the gap between words and everyday behaviour. No human economy company will achieve anything substantial for any length of time without all their people living and sharing their psyche, values, and virtues.

Take Four makes your wishbone happen.

'Force' recognises that no company is an island. Future success will depend on ensuring that whole value chains, or extended enterprises comprising several different companies, operate as a single unit to deliver agreed virtues collectively. 'Force' shows how to remove functional and organisational barriers.

Psyche

Information will shortly be available about all aspects of a company's behaviour, not just its products. Consumers are already grouping together to pool knowledge and increase their buying power. It will not be long before these groups will want to start influencing the behaviour of individual companies and even industries.

The relationship between corporations and consumers is about to change forever.

So what are you going to do about it?

You can, of course, wait and see. But get a life.

If failing to understand the importance of the Internet as a channel was a serious error a couple of years ago, failing to understand the way the Internet is going to change the balance of power between suppliers and consumers could prove fatal.

The impact of these market forces will drive a level of transparency into company behaviour that is still inconceivable today. The day of the 'consumer guerrilla' is not far away.

The analogy between companies and politicians is a good one. At the beginning of the 20th century, politicians could actually have a private life. Not so today – mass media changed all that. In a few years time the idea of companies being able to market brands willy-nilly, wherever they think there is a gap in the market, will seem bizarre.

Tomorrow's successful and sustainable companies will have to have visible integrity, and ensure that all their brands and their marketing programmes reflect their values and beliefs.

For any company contemplating life in the 21st century, understanding and communicating their unique identity is the biggest issue they must face.

the day of the 'consumer guerrilla' is not far away

Psychic Working

As I said in Scene One, achieving corporate karma will not be an option.

To maintain public and commercial confidence different types of company will have to evolve to deliver different types of brands. These are not absolutes but you will have to be clear about your primary focus, and the balance of all other factors.

You must ensure that this balance is not only reflected in all your actions but is recognised as doing so.

Psyche will help you establish just what your innate character as a company is.

Are you a benefit first, delivering satisfaction?

Or are you a virtual friend with a focus on customer delight?

Or are you a people company created to generate customer love?

For you to experience karma, psyche will help you check that all aspects of your organisation, your divisions, sectors, and brands are in harmony together reflecting the same Wishbone priorities.

Are you a people company created to generate customer love?

The psychic process

The core principle behind psyche is the need for human economy companies to focus or lose out. This focus is being forced on them by competitive pressure on the one hand, and corporate transparency along with increasing consumer demands on the other. Brand heroes are dead! Long live brand characters!

Is psyche easy to use?

Well, it's quick and it's visual.

Who can apply psyche?

Any individual, a board of directors, a whole management team, or even your competitors.

How can psyche be applied?

To a total organisation, or to a division. To an individual brand or group of brands. To your company or to a competitors.

Does psyche review actual behaviour or aspiration?

You can score it as you actually are, and how you would like to be.

Psyche won't produce tablets of stone, thank God! But it will make you think.

At the heart of the process is the new brand storm marketing mix and you will be asked to make priority decisions between different elements of the mix, from which will emerge the true nature of your organisation.

The main benefit of applying psyche will accrue when, in addition to applying the process at the top level of your organisation, you use it to assess different parts of your organisation, and apply it to your brand, or, if you trade with more than one, to all your brands. Comparison of the ensuing results will not only confirm your true nature but will tell you how consistent you are across your whole trading platform.

Psyche won't produce tablets of stone, thank God! But it will make you think

Step by step to psyche

Step one – Review the mix

Review the new marketing mix in the context of your organisation.

Step two – Score the mix

Once you have studied the mix in relation to your organisation it is time to score each element.

Step three – Create your psychic triangles

Either using the brand storm website or manually, create your psychic triangle.

Step four – Balance your organisation

Create and compare psychic triangles for each sector, region, and division in your organisation to see if they match. They should do.

Step five – Check your brand fit

Repeat the steps for each separate brand you own. Again, look for a close match.

Step six – Marry your talk to your walk

Check your brand and organisational triangles to see if there is a close fit. Now you can take action to ensure your organisation and brands are all singing off the same hymn sheet.

Step one – Review the mix

■ **Think about the *Brand Storm* marketing mix in relation to your company. You may think that all the elements are equally important, but for this exercise you are going to have to make some hard choices, for example, what is more important, your own people or being trusted by your customers? Start to prioritise each element.**

In my experience, just thinking about your company in this way will help as much as the results of the exercise.

You don't need to be a chief executive officer to do this, anybody can. Why not just do a first cut yourself and use the results to get other people thinking. Self-empowerment is the only way forward.

Capability: Your product performance

Just how good are your products? How reliable are they? How good are your guarantees? How much better are your products than the competitor's? Do you produce good functional, fit for purpose, market entry products? Do your products ooze quality and desirability? Do you have an established client base? How important are your products to your success?

Character: Your image

How powerful is your advertising? How strong is your brand name? How dynamic is your corporate identity? How good is your packaging? Are you a major sponsorship player? Does size matter? Do you foster product associations? How important is image to your success?

Care: Your service quality

How high are your customer service targets? Do you always exceed them? Have you got a service culture? Do your competitors benchmark their service against yours? How good is your customer service compared to other industries? Do you get a lot of complaints? Are customers who complain more or less loyal after you have dealt with their problem? Is your customer service a differentiater? Do you have service contracts directly or indirectly with your clients?

How important is customer service to your success?

Cost: Your value for money

Is your business price sensitive? Do you advertise your prices? Do your customers generally do price comparisons? Do they buy on price? Do you consistently check your competitor's prices? If your competitors change their prices, do you react? How important is your pricing strategy to your success?

Difference: Your individuality

Do you do similar things to others but in a different way? Are you always innovating? Do you have a distinct personality? Do you use technology differently to others? Are you unique? Can you easily be copied? Do you have a central role within a community group? How important to your success is being unique or different?

Delivery: Your convenience

Do you save your customers time? Do you offer global reach? Do you connect people with a joint interest? Does the value of your products vary quickly over time? Can you do things faster than others? Do you offer services that others can't? Do you deliver established things in a new form? Do you offer a wider range than others? Are you highly efficient? Are you reliable? How important is customer convenience to your success?

Delight: Your 'wow' factor

Do people interact with you? Is your product or service memorable? Are you always special? Do you always feature the latest hot craze? Will your customers' last experience be the reason they come back to you? Are you engaging? Are you more fun to do business with than your competitors? Are you entertaining or amusing? Are you a constant source of delight to your customers? How important to your success is emotionally engaging your customers?

Dynamics: Your 'buzz' factor

Do you have a powerful inspirational vision? Are you at the leading edge? Do you offer a new experience every day? Are you jamming? Are you cool? Do you give your customers today what others give them tomorrow? Are you funky? Do you rely on new technology to give you an advantage? Do others try and copy you? Are you always working on a new idea? Do you bring new groups of people together?

How important is change and continual evolution to your success?

People: Your human touch

Do people deliver your product? Do you have a large sales force? Are your people your product? Do live people heavily influence your customers? Are your people your most important asset? Is your customers' loyalty to your staff or to the company? Is recruitment a key challenge for you? Do your people reflect your values? Do you care about your people? Do your people care about you?

How important are your people to your success?

Partnership: Your network

Are you an island? Do you jointly meet your clients' needs with others? Are you part of an extended enterprise? Are you totally reliant on others to satisfy your customers? Do you actively seek partnership with others? Do you focus on delivering what you do best and let others do the rest? Are your partners your friends? Do your partners share your values and virtues?

How important is your network to your success?

Promise: Your integrity

Are there things more important to you than money? Are you passionate about your values? Do your customers buy from you because of your virtues? Do your values drive your strategy? Do all your stakeholders share and respect your values? Does respect for your values open up market opportunities to you that are closed to others? Do you always keep your promises?

How important to your success is keeping your promises?

Professionalism: Your reputation

Is your reputation paramount to you? Will you never let a customer down? Does your organisation have gravitas? Can you always be relied upon? Are you a byword for honesty? Do you have a network of partners and resources that are always there for you in times of need? Do you always do the right thing?

How important is trust to your success?

Step two — Score the mix

■ **Score each element of the brand storm marketing mix between one and 12.**

■ **Each score must be given only once.**

■ **Scoring should be based on the following:**

For assessing existing performance, the management time, priority and level of resource that element currently receives.

For creating an ideal scenario, the amount of time, priority, and resource it should receive.

For example:

Character	3
Capability	2
Care	7
Cost	4
Difference	12
Delivery	8
Delight	11
Dynamics	6
People	10
Partnership	1
Promise	5
Professionalism	9

■ **Allocate 12 bonus points to the element you scored highest, doubling its score to 24. This element should be the cornerstone of your psyche. In the above example, that means difference scores 24 (12+12).**

■ **Add up the total scores for each section, the Cs, the Ds and the Ps and then double each score.**

Step three — Create your psychic triangles

■ **Check that your total now adds up to 180.**

In our example that means:

C's score: **32:**   3 + 2 + 7 + 4 = 16 x 2 = **32**

D's score: **98:**   (12 x 2) + 8 + 11 + 6 = 49 x 2 = **98**

P's score: **50:**   10 + 1 + 5 + 9 = 25 x 2 = **50**

Total score: 180: 32 + 98 + 50 = **180**

■ **Each score determines the angle of one corner of your psychic triangle. These scores will determine your status as a benefit first based on the C's, virtual friend based on the D's or a people company based on the P's. They will also determine the relative importance of each of the other company types to your psyche.**

In our example, the company is strongly a virtual friend with secondary people company influence.

■ **Always position virtual friends at the top, benefit firsts to the left, and people company to the right.**

■ **Time to use a protractor to draw your own triangles.**

Link up with www.BrandStorm.com

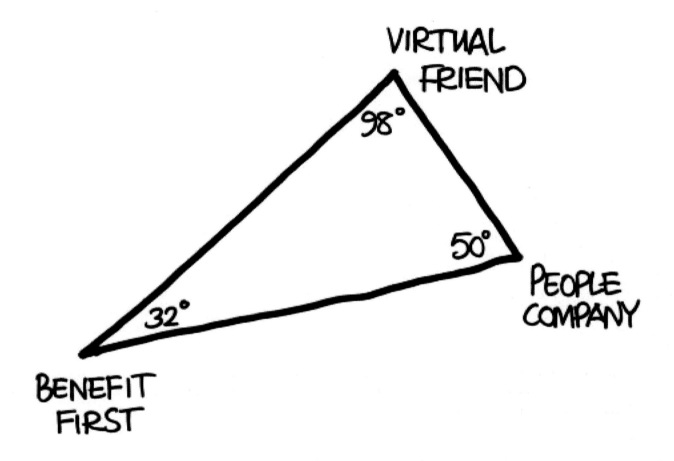

This is the psychic triangle from our example!

A virtual friend with secondary people company influence.

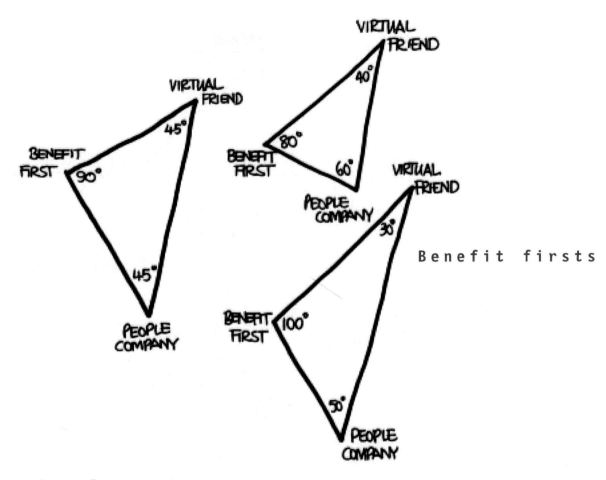

Benefit firsts

Love triangles

■ Interpret your triangles. Each shape will reflect a different corporate personality or psyche. The wider the angle of a corner the more dominant is that part of your Psyche.

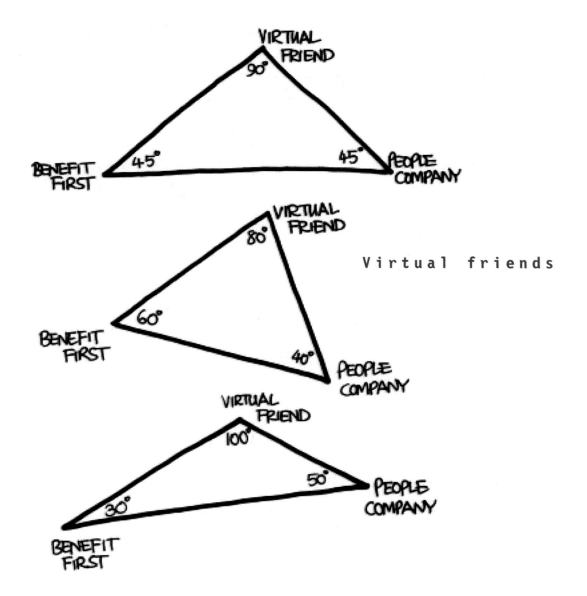

Virtual friends

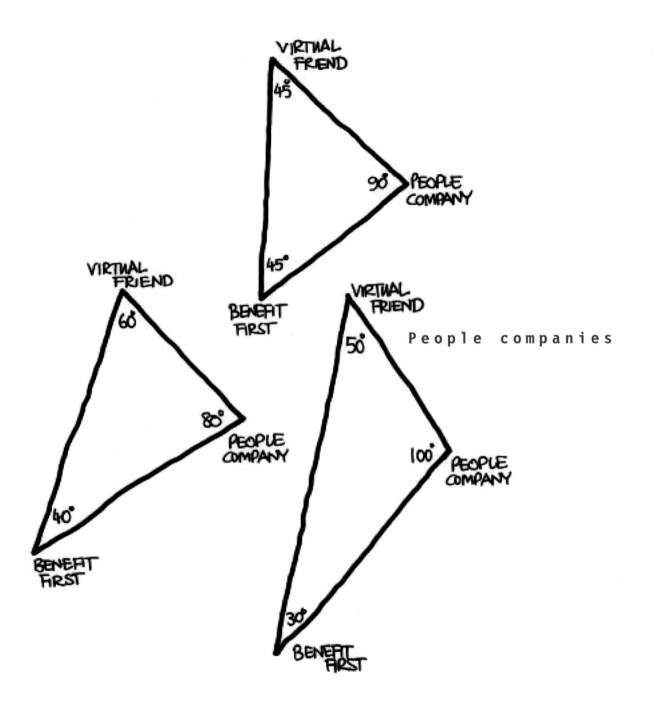

People companies

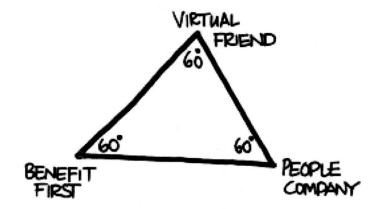

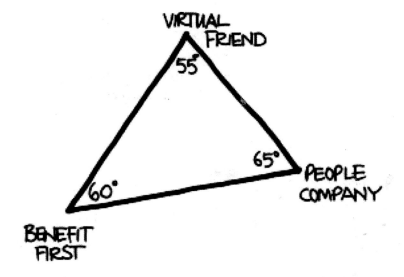

Egalitarians

- This is a toughie; all your angles are equal, or nearly equal. You have no clear psyche. It's time to start thinking about who you really want to be!

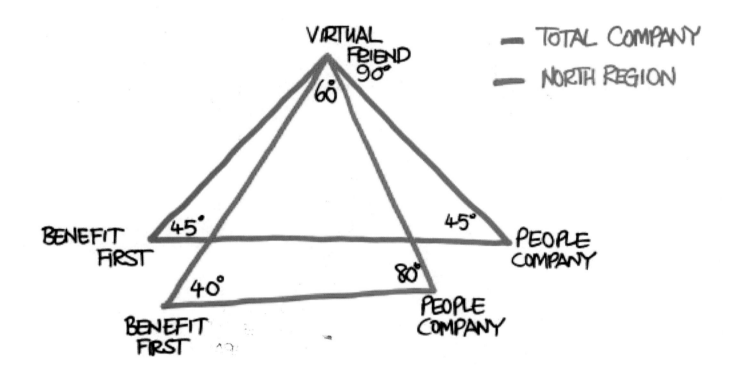

Step four – Balance your organisation

■ Repeat the last exercise for each meaningful operational team within your company, for example: sector, region, division, operating group, etc. Don't just compare your total section scores, but look closely at the balance within each section. This is vital.

■ Compare your organisational psychic triangles. Do they match? They should do!

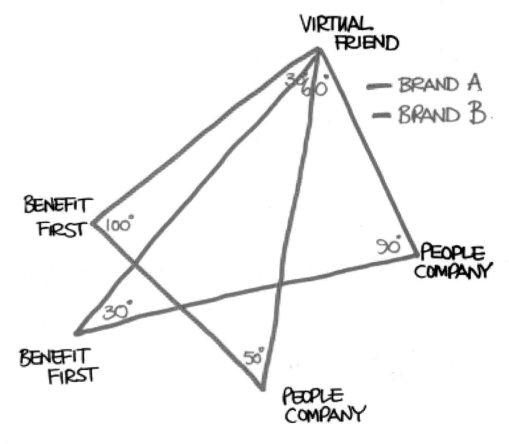

Step five – Check your brand fit

■ Repeat this exercise for every trading brand you manage. This time scores should be based not on management priority but, first, actual, and then desired, customer perception.

■ Do your brand triangles match?

Step six – Marry your talk to your walk

■ **Match up your organisational and brand triangles. How do they match?**

You now have all the information you need to bring your organisation together. If your organisational and brand triangles are misaligned or indistinct, it will cause corporate anxiety. Your corporate energy will be diffused and depleted. In short, you're suffering a corporate migraine.

■ **Decide what action you need to take, where to focus your effort, what to stop doing, and how big a task you actually face.**

If your organisational and brand triangles are misaligned you'll suffer organisational anxiety and a corporate migraine

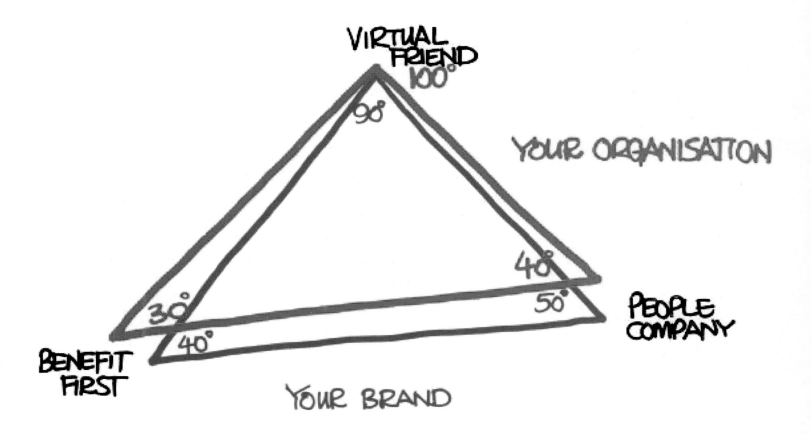

VIRTUAL
FRIEND
100°

98°

YOUR ORGANISATION

40°

30°

50°

BENEFIT
FIRST

40°

PEOPLE
COMPANY

YOUR BRAND

Corporate transparency, consumer demands, and tigerlike competition will force you to focus or die.

Don't be all things to all men.

Make tough choices.

Work out who you want to be.

Be the best at it.

Do it wholeheartedly.

Match your own behaviour with your brand talk or suffer a corporate migraine.

Psyche unifies your ideas, actions, and brands.

Spirit

If you have already completed 'Psyche' you should by now have a clear wishbone, and a sense of your vision, identity, and marketing priorities. In 'Spirit', I want to build on this.

For most people, having a vision of their future will be critical. But, if you are unclear about how you will achieve your vision, you are as likely to fail as if you have no vision at all. The ultimate determinant of your success, whatever business you are in, will always be your brand.

When I use the word brand, I do not mean it in the narrow sense of a visual device; I am talking about it as the embodiment of your customers' complete and continuing relationship with you.

The future, rather than signalling the end of brands, as some people have forecast, will herald the need for stronger, more robust, and complete brands than ever. Brands with total integrity as was discussed in 'Psyche'.

Think customer, then multiply it by 100!

The majority of human economy brands will be founded on relationships with customers not dreamed up in ad agencies. To achieve this, you will need a degree of customer understanding and empathy previously unseen.

Achieving empathy will not be easy and it only gets good when your customers empathise with you. If your customers don't like you, you ain't coming in!

Spirit is made up of two key elements:

Brand spirit which, as the name suggests, looks at your brand's performance in the market place.

Customer spirit, concentrating on how to imbed customer focus, and a real interest in your customers, into your psyche and wishbone.

If your customers don't like you, you ain't coming in!

Being OK isn't OK

In this age of unprecedented competition, just being out there and being OK won't do. Gone are the days of local geographic monopolies and cosy local cartels. If your products aren't delightful, there are colleges full of dotcom teenagers just panting to get at your customers and it's never been easier for them to do so.

It's a tough old world, and it won't get any easier. Unless you are totally genuine, care deeply about your customers, are truly the best at what you do, and are genuinely different, your days are numbered. The upside, though, is that there has never been a better time to challenge preconceptions and try something new.

If you have an established marketing department you will already have measures in place to track your brand's performance, and, hopefully, your customer satisfaction. The brand and customer focus tests in 'Spirit' are not designed to replace these existing measures but to complement them. The information you have already obtained will be a useful input into your work on 'Spirit'.

'Spirit' is a quick litmus test that can be used by anyone (marketing teams, CEOs, finance guys or individual entrepreneurs), at any time, to keep the key issues of brand performance and customer focus front of mind.

Every couple of months try them out again. Are your scores going up? Which bits have changed? Try the tests on different parts of the organisation. What do sales think? How about your call centre team?

Customer focus and your brand performance are not just a marketing issue. They impact on everyone in the organisation because they drive your success. Make sure that everyone has a role to play in their continuing development.

If your whole organisation is not constantly thinking about your customers and your brands, your competitors will be!

There are colleges full of dotcom teenagers just panting to get at your customers

Enter the spirit world

Benchmarks for success are not only lifting, they are changing. The traditional measures of brand awareness and brand perception are still valid but are only part of the picture. To understand your brand's position in your market and how it is likely to fare going forward, you need to create a more holistic view.

Alongside how well known your brand is, other brand considerations need to be considered:

What is the power of your brand outside your traditional market area?

Is your brand seen as having integrity?

What role does it play in your customers' lives?

Would the quality of their lives be diminished without your product or service?

Do your customers see your brand as a standalone item or part of an ongoing relationship with your company?

Do your customers really care about your brand or can they take it or leave it?

Do you know the answers? If so, how do you know?

Do you measure these things?

Do you regularly review the answers?

Do you ask different parts of your organisation the same questions?

Don't ever settle for one view; ask everyone, particularly if they speak to customers. Create an environment where your whole organisation see your brand as their baby and want to nurture it.

Many of the successful brands in the human economy will take on a life of their own; they will have their own personalities, their own spirit. They will engage with their customers in a variety of ways, both real and remote, and will have their own friends and associations. These are the brands that will last longest in the market place, evolving and changing, incorporating new technologies and innovations both into the actual products and services delivered, and into the means of delivering them. The personality and spirit of these brands will transcend the actual products and services they represent.

In the new brand world, just as in life, the most attractive brands must avoid becoming narcissistic. **Less focus on brand associations, more on brand relationships. Less advertising, more delivery. Less introvert, more extrovert.**

Tomorrow's brands must stop being product champions and become consumer companions

Fair's fair

A key part of success is also ambition. How much do you want to win and keep winning? How high are your standards and your expectations? If you try either brand spirit or customer spirit you will be surprised at how hard it is to get a reasonable score. This is not accidental. If you aim low you will achieve low. Most brand and customer service targets are far too low to achieve any real improvement in the brand's fortune. Customer service or brand perception scores of seven or eight out of ten are only mediocre. Average scores must be consistently well over nine out of ten to deserve loyalty from your customers.

If this seems unfair or unrealistic, let's put it into context. How many times have you experienced outstanding service? When you are trying to check into a hotel, enjoy a meal out, sort out a phone bill, return a faulty item to a shop or order an item over the Internet? Average service in the world today is just that, average. In fact, if you ask me it's worse than that, it's crap!

And it is not significantly a geographic thing. In many cases, it's as bad in the USA as it is in Europe. In fact, on a recent comparison of service in Disney Stores around the world I found the best, not in America, but in London.

It's also fair to say that, on many occasions, service is getting worse. Technology is putting up more and more barriers. How many times do you try getting through to your own automated call handling system? How many CEOs haven't installed an automated call handling system between them and their team, yet think that it is good enough for their customers? Can you remember seeing loads of reserved parking places right in front of the door when you have been visiting as a client and you have to park around the corner? How did it make you feel? Not great, I guess.

I got angry at a train station recently when there were several empty but reserved staff parking places in front of the station and the customer car park was miles away. When I complained to the stationmaster, he told me in all seriousness that it was too dangerous to ask staff to park down the end of the car park. I rest my case.

How many examples of poor service can you think of? I know I could quite happily go on all day. How many examples of fantastic service that shot your expectation to bits can you recall? Not so many I would think.

Poor service is naturally endemic for the simple reason that people have been able to get away with it so far. Well, not for much longer. With the choice available to your customers, they won't accept second rate or average any more. And they now have the power to do something about it. Good service is not that hard to deliver. In many cases, it is a question of attitude rather than expense. You do, of course, need to create the right culture and it needs to be led from the top.

How many CEOs haven't installed an automated call handling system between them and their team, yet think that it is good enough for their customers?

It's in my nature

You can't achieve anything for your customers unless you are always thinking about them and talking to them.

There is an old adage: if you can't measure it don't do it. Unfortunately, when it comes to customer focus, not doing it is not an option. So, I've created customer spirit. Like the other models in *Brand Storm*, it is not rocket science, but it will give you a framework to regularly consider just how focused your organisation is on your customers.

Customer spirit looks at several aspects of how you operate, and of your relationship with your customers. It then asks you to consider both how important they are to you and how well you perform in those areas:

- Do your customers set your customer satisfaction measures?

- Are all your staff rewarded on customer satisfaction performance?

- Do you give your customers the benefit of the doubt?

- Do you revere your customer-facing staff?

At the heart of customer spirit is your attitude to your customers. Do you really care about them or are your customers a necessary evil? It is no good just implementing a new change team for the masses and hoping it will work.

Having an exceptional customer spirit will make you an exceptional organisation. Still very few companies have got it. Having seen exceptional service deliver exceptional results, I don't fully understand why this is so. I do believe, though, that many companies forget that first and foremost, they are in the service business, and focus on products, technology or shareholders, and therefore neglect their customer spirit. Having no established measurement does not help either. How many times is your customer spirit discussed at the team meetings you attend?

Just as a matter of interest, are you personally fanatical about your customers or is the next organisational change, promotion or corporate politics more important?

The great news is that almost anyone can start a spirit revolution if they are passionate about their customers. Used together brand and customer spirit can be your company health check. Use them and light the blue touch paper.

Are you fanatical about your customers?

Get in the spirit

Is spirit easy to use?

Dead easy, it is only a simple test, and you can try it on the train or as a full corporate exercise. Every step is supported by the brand storm website.

Link up to www.BrandStorm.com

Who can apply spirit?

Anyone, a board of directors, a whole management team or even your competitors. Just do it! If your spirit is weak, your customers will come back and haunt you!

How can spirit be applied?

Brand spirit can be applied to any trading or corporate brand. Customer spirit can be applied at total organisation or any divisional level.

Does spirit review actual behaviour or aspiration?

It was originally designed to review existing brands or organisations but there is no reason why you could not use it as part of your wishbone process to create aspirations, performance against which can actually be measured.

If your spirit is weak, your customers will come back and haunt you!

Step by step to brand spirit

Step one – Review your brand attributes
Review and agree the top ten brand attributes for your organisation.

Step two – Score your performance
Look at each attribute and score your performance.

Step three – Rate their importance
Look at each attribute and rate their performance from vital (9), highly important (8), to important to your organisation (7).

Step four – Calculate your total brand strength
Use the Brand Spirit formula to calculate your total brand strength.

Step five – Rate your market importance
How great is your ambition? Look at how high you set the bar.

Step six – Action stations
Now you have the information, what action should you take?

The brand spirit survey

Brand spirit is designed to measure the power of your brand in the market place.

Link up with www.BrandStorm.com

Step one – Review your brand attributes

- **Brand spirit works by prioritising and scoring a list of ten brand attribute questions. Ideally, these should be tailored to your specific situation but to kick the process off here are ten which will generally be appropriate and can be used to start your debate. Use them or change them but agree your ten chosen attributes.**

Example brand attributes

Is your brand incredibly well known?

An oldie but a goodie. This is always a great place to start. However wonderful everything you do is, if people don't know about it, then it's all a waste of time. If you don't already have awareness targets that are regularly reviewed by your whole management team, sort them out today.

Are you the most desired brand in your class?

Well, you should be. This is not all about cost or being a premium brand it is about being cool and desirable. Think of it this way: the best looking people are definitely not always the sexiest.

Is your brand perceived as outstanding value in its class?

I'm not talking cheap here, guys. I'm talking outstanding value. Why shouldn't you be outstanding value? Your customers deserve it and if you are not, you can bet your bottom dollar someone else will be. Oh, and by the way, let's not start thinking prices; start thinking value. Give your customers a better overall experience, serve them better, care more, and listen more. Love them.

There is a critical issue here too. Make sure you give them the things they value, not just the things they want, or you're going broke! (Do you know what they value?)

Does your brand have loyal, regular customers?

The key word here is loyal, not regular. I use the train regularly but I'm not loyal; in fact, I hate it. Give me an alternative, and I'm off. So will your customers be if you're not careful.

In all the work I have carried out looking at the correlation between customer satisfaction and loyalty, the only time you get genuine loyalty is when you use satisfaction measures set by the customer, and you start scoring well in excess of nine out of ten all the time. Your customers' expectations will be constantly rising, and never faster than now. Today's exceptional experience is tomorrow's expectation.

Does your brand flourish outside your own core business?

This is a cool test for a brand. The most powerful brands can all transfer from their own market to another. How would your brand fare? Could it be used on perfume? On clothes? On cars? As an Internet portal?

Do people trust your brand (trust you)?

This is a biggie. Trust is the most important issue in the human economy. Brands will soon be treated just like people. You will become a friend, an acquaintance, a lover, or an ex. If you ever want to be more than just an acquaintance, trust will be crucial.

Are your brands easy to get hold of?

Obvious but, nonetheless, important. With more channels of communication opening up, you have never had more choice about how to connect with your customer. Of course, similarly, your customer has never had as many diversions. With expectations rising, problems in the delivery of your service or problems communicating with you will kill you. Ease of consumer access is now a market entry criterion.

Today's exceptional customer experience is tomorrow's expectation

Are your products and brand really innovative?

This will be more important to some than others but innovation should be considered in the context of total customer experience and not just product experience. In the human economy even tradition must be innovative.

Do your customers promote your brand to their friends and colleagues?

This is always the way to separate the men from the boys. You have probably all read that people with a complaint against a company tell ten people while those who are pleased tell only a couple. Well, this is not always the case. If you can absolutely blow your customers away with the way you treat them, they will tell everyone.

This is not limited to service companies either; whatever you do, whether it is selling gravel, making sweets or supplying industrial parts, if you are exceptional, people will talk about it.

OK, so it is easy for me to say 'be exceptional'. What do I think you have been trying to do anyway? Well, I don't think the answer is doing more things. It is about focus, it is about listening to customers, and it is about delivering what your customers value, not just what they want. But most important it's about your perceived attitude towards your customers. New consumers won't tolerate people taking the piss, even if they deliver.

Is your brand part of your customers' lives?

This is a major test for a brand. Particularly if you aspire to customer love. People do not love things that are not an integral part of their everyday thoughts. What would happen if you closed down today?

Would your customers mourn you?

How would your obituary read?

Would you be sadly missed?

Who would cry for you?

Would your customers mourn you? How would your obituary read?

Step two – Score your performance

■ Now that you have selected and agreed your final list of attribute questions, score each attribute out of ten, based on either the current performance of, or your aspiration for, your brand.

Step three – Score the importance

■ Score the importance of each factor between seven and nine based on each individual market situation. Nine is vital, eight is highly important, and seven is important.

Step four – Calculate your total brand strength

■ Subtract your importance scores from performance scores to arrive at your gross brand attribute scores. These scores may be positive or negative.

■ Multiply importance score and gross brand attribute score to arrive at total brand attribute scores.

■ Add up total brand attribute scores (both positive and negative) to calculate total brand strength score.

Use the Brand Storm website to talk to other people implementing the brand storm models. Share ideas on how to personally make a difference and ignite enthusiasm in your organisation.

If you identify further brand attributes, use the website to share them with other brand storm pioneers. *Brand Storm* is a living interactive book and will come even more to life for you when you interact with others.

Discuss your experiences at www.BrandStorm.com

Here is a worked example of how your brand spirit results might look:

Brand attributes	Brand performance score	Market importance	Total score
Is your brand incredibly well known?	10	9 = 1	9
Are you the most desired brand in your class?	6	9 = −3	−27
Is your brand perceived as outstanding value in its class?	9	7 = 2	14
Does your brand have loyal, regular customers?	8	8 = 0	0
Does your brand flourish outside your own core business?	6	7 = −1	−7
Is your brand seen as having integrity?	6	8 = −2	−16
Are your brands easy to get hold of?	9	7 = 2	14
Are your products and brand really innovative?	10	7 = 3	21
Do your customers promote your brand to their friends and colleagues?	7	7 = 0	0
Is your brand part of your customers' lives?	4	8 = −4	−32

Total brand strength = -24
Total market importance = 77

Total brand strength

As you can see in this example, getting a top total brand strength score is not easy. If you look at the individual brand performance scores they were not bad. Two tens, two nines, an eight, a seven, three sixes, and one poor score of four. The resultant total brand score of only −24 was, however, very disappointing.

As I said earlier, being OK isn't OK any more!

You should be aiming for a total brand strength score of 70 or more. Anything less is cause for concern.

Discuss your experience at: www.BrandStorm.com

Step five – Total market importance

This is the total of all your individual market importance scores. In our example, the score was 77. The maximum score achievable is 100, if you score each brand attribute equally at ten.

Your ambition and degree of customer focus will drive up your total market importance score. The higher the score, the greater the challenge you are setting yourself.

- **Review your score; is it high enough? Not all the brand attributes will be, or should ever be, totally equal, but a target of at least 90 is not a bad idea.**

Step six – Action stations

OK, so now you have a view of how strong your brand is, or, if you are in a start-up situation, how strong you would like it to be, you can start to take action.

Again, as on many occasions in this book, the answer is focus. By choosing the ten most important brand attributes to start with you will have started to focus. Now it is time to focus further still.

- **Look at your bottom line total brand strength score. Is it negative? Have you broken into positive? Have you hit the important 70 mark? Are you soaring up near the 100 point? Do you have cause for concern or is it time for Champagne?**

- **Look individually at any high positive and high negative brand attribute scores. High negatives are clearly areas of concern. High positives are also important as they may indicate wasted effort and lack of focus.**

- **Study relative scores looking for any that may conflict with the achievement of another brand attribute.**

- **To achieve greatest brand improvement, focus your management effort and organisational resources on your three lowest and two highest scoring brand attributes. Develop action plans for these involving the whole company and plan to review in three months' time.**

Step by step to customer spirit

Step one – Review your customer spirit

Review and agree the top ten customer spirits for your organisation.

Step two – Score your performance

Look at each spirit and score your performance.

Step three – Rate their importance

Look at each spirit and rate their performance from vital (9), highly important (8), to important to your organisation (7).

Step four – Calculate your total customer spirit

Use the customer spirit formula to calculate your total customer spirit.

Step five – Rate your customer importance

How great is your ambition? Look at how high you set the bar.

Step Six – Action stations

Now you have the information, what action should you take?

Having considered the current strength of your brand, let's now look at the likelihood of maintaining and improving your brand position. The second stage of spirit, is customer spirit. Like the rest of brand storm, customer spirit is not a universal panacea, but a framework for considering and measuring customer focus that will give you a head start in any market.

Use it or weep.

Step one – Review your customer spirits

Link up with: www.BrandStorm.com

- Using the same type of methodology used for brand spirit, we can examine the customer spirit within your brand. Again, here is a list of possible customer spirits. Use it as it is, change some of the spirits to fit your own market scenario, or develop your own list. If you come up with interesting new ideas use the website and share them. Don't forget to compare the view of different functions and departments within your organisation.

- Agree your ten chosen customer spirits.

Example customer spirit

Are you totally passionate about customers?

We are not talking mildly interested here, we are talking do you bleed when your customers bleed? Would you give them your last chocolate?

Passion is a hard thing to quantify, unless it's being done to you, then you know. Ask your customers whether they think you are passionate about them, at least you will get some interesting answers. Ask your team what they think being passionate about your customers means. Ask them who in the organisation they think is passionate about customers. Once identified, promote them. Identify what makes these people special and foster it. Build it into your selection process.

Be passionate yourself. Passion breeds passion

Do you know in detail who your customers are and what they want?

Basic, but still relevant. The more you know about your customers the better, and it has never been easier to learn about them. The key, as in so many things, is still, however, asking the right questions and listening to what is said, not just what you want to hear. The days of A, B, C1, C2 etc., are pretty much gone but what to replace it with? Try to learn things your competitors are not even thinking about, and use it to your advantage.

Do your customers set your satisfaction and brand performance measures?

I am continually surprised at how little imagination goes into the construction of satisfaction measurement reporting. Let your customers lead the way. Each will have different needs and expectations. If the things you are working on are worthy but unvalued, you're wasting time and money and, in a more competitive environment, may go under.

If you have a relatively small number of customers, develop individual measurements for each one. If you work in a mass market make it fun and easy for your customers to contact you and reward them for doing so. Beware legacy measures, just because you measured that last time don't measure it again without asking why.

Do all your managers regularly talk to customers?

Not do some of your managers, do *all* your managers talk to customers on a regular basis? Any manager in your organisation who hasn't spoken in detail to a customer he didn't previously know in the last month is stagnating and may well be damaging your company. Think about it.

Any manager not regularly talking to customers is actively damaging your organisation

Is everyone encouraged to understand your brand satisfaction information?

This is an important cultural point. If people think that the marketing department alone owns responsibility for your brands and customer satisfaction they won't get involved in new ideas and developments. Involvement must be encouraged, it must be facilitated, and it must be informed. Everyone should be concentrating on customers, everyone should have a view, and everyone should be listened to.

Your whole organisation should be well versed in your brand and customer satisfaction targets and performance. They should be enabled to take a pride in your performance and a share of your successes.

Do you encourage and trust customer feedback and take brand action on it?

What can you honestly say you do to encourage customers to talk to you, not when you want to ask them something but when they have something to say?

There is an untapped gold mine out there. This is very relevant if you are trading remotely over the net or using an agency or bureau call centre. The more remote you are from your customer, the harder you must work to hear what they have to say.

Do you benchmark customer reaction to competitor brands?

You probably don't have a monopoly on your customers. Do you know how they feel about your competitors' total performance? Do you know which brands your customers love in other markets and why?

Do you revere and listen to your customer-handling staff?

Your customer-facing staff are your most vital asset. Do they feel it? Have you asked them? It is very hard to make a customer feel loved if you feel lonely and abused yourself.

Write down five things that you do now to make your customer team feel loved and special.

It is very hard to make a customer feel loved if you feel lonely and abused yourself

Are all your staff rewarded on customer satisfaction and brand performance?

Some things are so important that everyone should have a stake in the game. This is one of them. Ensure that every member of your company is paid, at least in part, based on customer satisfaction and brand performance, and your satisfaction will go up.

Do your senior managers, your NBD team, your finance, HR, and strategy people work one week a year in a customer-facing role?

It is about attitude. If all your key staff are not spending a meaningful amount of consolidated time with customers, how can they be doing their job right?

Without meaningful time in front of customers how can:

A board member set strategy?

A marketer develop new products?

A finance manager make the right decisions?

An HR manager help recruit the right people?

Step two – Score your performance

■   **Score each customer spirit between one and ten, based either on your perception of your current performance or, if you are in a start-up situation, use it to set targets for your future performance.**

It is useful in any situation to use customer spirit as a target-setting device. You can never take customer focus for granted. You can never score too high. You can conduct a customer spirit survey on your own, as a quick test, or it is ideal for debate at team meetings or awaydays.

Link up with www.BrandStorm.com

■   **If you have several trading divisions carry out a customer spirit exercise for each one.**

Step three – Rate their importance

■ Once you have scored your performance for each spirit, score the relative importance of each spirit to you. Score each spirit between seven and nine based on your individual situation. Nine is vital, eight is highly important and seven important.

Step four – Calculate your total customer spirit

■ Subtract your importance scores from your performance scores to arrive at gross customer spirit scores. These scores may be positive or negative.

■ Multiply importance scores and gross customer spirit scores to arrive at individual total customer spirit scores.

■ Add up individual spirit scores (positive and negative) to calculate total customer strength score.

Use the Brand Storm website to talk to other people implementing customer spirit. Share ideas on how you can personally make a difference and ignite enthusiasm in your organisation for adopting the brand storm principles.

If you experience any problems applying customer spirit share them with other users on the web who may have an answer.

When you create new customer focus attributes, share them. *Brand Storm* is a living, interactive, book that will come even more to life when you interact with other users.

Here is a worked example of how your customer spirit results might look:

Customer spirits	Customer performance score	Market importance	Total score
Are you totally passionate about customers?	6	9 = −3	−27
Do you know in detail who your customers are and what they want?	8	8 = 0	0
Do your customers set your satisfaction and brand performance measures?	3	9 = −6	−54
Do all your managers regularly talk to customers?	6	7 = −1	−7
Is everyone encouraged to understand your brand satisfaction information?	8	7 = 1	7
Do you encourage and trust customer feedback and take brand action on it?	9	8 = 1	8
Do you benchmark customer reaction to competitor brands?	7	7 = 0	0
Do you revere and listen to your customer handling staff?	6	9 = −3	−27
Are all staff rewarded on customer satisfaction and brand performance?	7	7 = 0	0
Do your senior managers, your NBD teamy our finance, HR and strategy people work one week a year in customer-handling roles?	2	8 = −6	−48

Total customer strength = -148
Total customer importance = 79

Total customer strength

As was the case with brand spirit, achieving a top total customer strength score is not easy. The individual customer spirit scores were just about reasonable overall but let down badly by two scores. A nine, two eights, two sevens, three sixs, a poor three, and a dreadful two. The resultant total customer strength of –148 would be a real worry.

- **Aim for a minimum score of 70 for starters, anything less is a major cause for concern. If you are scoring less than 95, competitors out there are stealing your customers.**

Discuss your experience at: www.BrandStorm.com

Step five – Rate your customer importance

Total customer importance is the total of all your individual market importance scores. In our example, the score was 79. The maximum score achievable is 100, if you score each brand attribute equally at ten.

Remember your ambition and degree of customer focus will drive up your total market importance score. The higher the score, the greater the challenge you are setting yourself.

As with brand spirit, not all the attributes will be, or should be, totally equal, but a target of over 90 is appropriate.

- **Check your individual market importance scores and review your total customer importance.**

Step six – Action stations

Having carried out customer spirit, you will now have a clear idea of how fit your customer focus is. If you are in good shape, you must keep it that way, and make customer focus endemic to your culture. If you have a customer gap, it is time to fill it.

At the risk of sounding boring, it is time for more focus. By choosing the ten most important customer focus attributes to start with, you will have started to focus. Now it is the time to focus further still.

- **Look at your bottom line total brand strength score. Is it negative? Have you broken into positive? Have you hit the important 70 mark? Are you soaring up near the 100 point?**

- **Look individually at any high positive and high negative attribute scores. High negatives are clearly areas of concern. High positives are also important as they may indicate wasted effort.**

- **To achieve the greatest customer focus improvement, concentrate on your three lowest and two highest scoring attributes. Develop action plans for these involving the whole company and plan to review these in three months' time.**

Put your best foot forward

What you do now should be a no-brainer.

It is unarguable that you need a strong brand in the market place. It is unarguable that the tighter your customer focus, the better you will perform. Doing it right makes more money.

Spirit is not some deeply scientific model for valuing brands or customer focus. It is a simple pragmatic commonsense framework to enable you to do what is right for your organisation, and your market. Hopefully, it will remove any complacency and stimulate you to think creatively about your brands, and the way you consider your customers. It definitely provides a framework for reviewing progress. Your market and your customers never stop changing. Don't let them out of your sight for even a second.

Think, eat, sleep, breath customer

To succeed in the human economy, you need robust, honest, and complete customer-centric brands.

Be a customer fanatic.

Be totally involving.

Be consistent.

Be different.

Be truly desirable.

Don't take the piss.

Stop being a product champion. Become a consumer companion.

Spirit puts your customers and brands first.

Life

The picture should be building by now. You know who you want to be and how to unify your brand pitch to your own behaviour. You are fanatical about your customers and your brands. Now it's time to make sure you can bring your whole team with you.

No care no share

It is impossible to achieve any significant goals in life without working as part of a team. This isn't just a work thing, it applies to virtually any part of life. Whether the team you belong to is your family, a sports team or a community group, co-operation is essential. Can you imagine a couple of guys with a great idea building the pyramids one afternoon, or the Panama Canal, or the Great Wall of China? Even things that appear to be personal achievements are, these days, a team effort. You cannot win an Olympic medal without a team to support, train, and motivate you. The production of this book would not have been possible without contributors, designers, editors, and a publisher, etc.

What makes someone choose to be part of a team? Outside work, people usually have a choice and only opt in if they want to. There is usually some common purpose that unites people to work together. You don't join a theatre group if you don't want to be in the production. You don't join a football team if you don't want to play football.

At work it is a bit different. Opting in or out is not an option. You are part of a team because you're bloody well told to be! And if you don't like it you know what you can do!

Some companies still seem quite happy to behave like this and expect to get away with it. In fact, in the 1980's it was pretty standard procedure. But not any more, now it is less 'no pain no gain' more 'no care no share'.

And what has changed to bring about this miracle? Put simply, it is choice: consumer choice, media choice, community choice, employment choice. In the human economy, teamwork is based on respect, being the best, and being fair.

Can you imagine a couple of guys with a great idea building the pyramids one afternoon?

Vision relief

To make teams gel in a purely work context you need to create the same compelling desire to achieve a single vision, or satisfy a single need, that exists in non-work teams. This is not always straightforward, however.

Non-work teams will be naturally vision orientated. It's the primary reason you sign up, you work together to save the planet, because you all collect stamps, or to fight famine in Africa. Even then maintaining co-operation is a full-time job.

Most business organisations have no natural vision orientation. Can you imagine it, I want to work here to save the world's fax machine population, or bring toilet paper to the world's bottoms. I want to commute to work every day, eat in a canteen, and be put under stress. Actually, now that I think about it, how about this for vision motivation:

'I want to spend my whole life designing machines to make work easier, less boring and less stressful for office workers. I want to start work when I'm 18. I want to get up at six every morning and work through to six at night, for 50 weeks a year. I never want to see my wife or kids and I want to retire at sixty plus when I'm worn out and have no interests outside work!'

That might be a slightly bleak picture of work in your organisation but, certainly until recently, it represented life for many, many people. No wonder so much service is crap, so many processes are poorly engineered, and so many customers and employees dissatisfied.

Man cannot live on vision alone

In the human economy people want a life. They want to be part of something, they want to wear whatever they feel like, they want to feel special, and they want to have fun. They even want time doing something other than work. The most amazing thing is that they can. People can now create and live their own 'business-style'.

If your work sensation does not compete, the only people you will attract tomorrow are the leftovers, the people who haven't got what it takes, or who cannot be bothered, to take control of their lives.

Less work station more work sensation

Lose the remote control

If you want the best people, create an environment they will want to be in. Make it fun, make it immersive, make it flexible, make it inspiring. Create a business-style business. Bin the standard contracts, you're buying people, not parts. Give them the type of things they would want if they worked for themselves.

The chance to make a real difference

Support ideas. Support risk takers. The number of companies that say they do this but actually don't is staggering. In big legacy businesses people progress by not being offensive. The mediocre still float to the top. With the length of the average strategic plan dropping from five years in the 1980's to 12 months now, rapid action, not careful planning, is the key. The Fourth Room, the UK strategic marketing consultancy I used to work for, had the motto 'leap before you look'. Go wild, take a flier, and give it a try.

International opportunity

Working internationally is a great eye opener. Make it happen, inspiring them helps you.

Part-time working

Welcome to the two-day, three-day, four-day week. Bring in the three-week month. If they want a sabbatical, give them one. If they don't feel fresh, they are losing you money. How about duvet days – two or three days a year where if a person can't get out of bed, they don't have to? Let that person ring in and claim one of their duvet days, without resorting to a sick–note mentality. Many of today's corporate working practices weren't created last century, they were created two centuries ago. Chuck them out.

Networking opportunities

When people talk about the networked economy they are generally talking computers. The real networking that is setting the world alight is not computers, though, it's people. Computers facilitate, people propagate. In the human economy, get your people talking. It's fun, it's funky, it's fresh.

Support for their family and interests

You want people to get involved in your business, so get involved in their life. Take an interest in their interests, have family events.

Bin the standard contracts, you're buying people, not parts

How virtuous is that?

If part of the picture is about a cool business environment, the second part is about creating meaning, and something people can relate to. If you can't use your vision to do that, what can you use? You guessed it, your values and virtues!

Everyone knows about values. Once you've got a vision statement, get some values. The problem is that most are poorly communicated, not bought into and rarely generate anything, let alone action.

This is not a great surprise. The only company values that I have ever bought into are ones I have been involved in creating. That is the issue. Values are great for stirring up discussion but are hard to live and even harder to measure. Unless your values and beliefs are turned into meaningful everyday behaviours, your staff cannot embrace them. Unless you create living and identifiable virtues, your customers will never experience them.

Hello life, come on down

Life adds virtues to values. It introduces a process for reviewing both overall corporate and individual performance against your agreed values and virtues. It is about letting your people share and live your psyche in an open and measurable way, allowing customers to become immersed in your brand.

There are a great number of powerful reasons for having agreed, open and measurable organisational values.

If you want people to follow in your footsteps, wear the shoes you want filled, or something like that, you get the gist. Company leaders must be seen to live the same identified behaviours they want their company to live. You can't behave one way and expect everyone to follow what you say, ignoring what you do. In fact, not only should your behaviour be beyond reproach but your team should have every chance to examine and comment on your behaviour.

Your people are your company's greatest asset. They need performance management. They should reflect your brand message. If you want to develop and grow this asset both as individuals and as a cultural group you must create a system for doing so. Many companies just publish their values and hope. If that is what you do, your chances of making any noticeable cultural progress are negligible. Your team's ability to live your psyche must be measurable and reviewable as individuals, while your overall company performance must be auditable.

This is not a one-way thing. It is not about saying, 'we do it like this round here, so get on with it.' It is not about producing the *Stepford Wives*. It is about making sure that your customers' contact with your people lives comfortably with their brand expectation. It also means the functions within the company, from finance and HR to logistics and new product development, will strengthen your brand rather than harm it. It is about brand strength, not strong-arm tactics.

If you want people to follow in your footsteps, wear the shoes you want filled

Two become one

It is widely believed that behavioural compatibility is the most likely factor to impact on the success of any corporate merger or acquisition. If you understand your own behaviour and can analyse the behaviour of others against the same criteria you can start to predict the outcome of any potential merger. In an environment where brand integrity is paramount, mergers and acquisitions will need to be reviewed far more carefully. Brand and cultural fit will rapidly rise in importance or the risk of damage to both brands may be considerable.

Clear brand and cultural expression will also be the first line of defence in the face of unwanted attention. If you can show strong cultural and brand misalignment, you can take the heart of anyone's attack.

Hey, good looking!

Have you tried recruiting for good staff recently? it is not easy. Less than 20 percent of people have the skill required for more than 80 percent of new economy jobs. Those with the right skills coupled with the right attitudes to fit your brand will be few and far between.

With more and more career choices, potential recruits are increasingly looking for evidence of a company's culture and behaviours as the critical decision factor in which firm they join. This brings a new dimension to the battle to attract new team members. Straightforward financial and contractual factors will not be sufficient to attract the most attractive candidates. They will be looking for holistic, emotionally embracing career openings.

From your perspective, it means you need to be a lot choosier too. Every time you make a mistake with one of your living brand representatives, you damage your brand.

Hopefully, using life will improve your recruitment and help you make fewer mistakes.

Island hopping

If there are powerful arguments for having clear values and virtues within a company, this is only half the story. No successful company in the human economy will be an island. Those organisations that succeed in making their values and virtues live through their partners, as well as in themselves, will really start to cook on gas.

The life process can help you pick the right partners in the first place and provide a framework for assessing how well they are living your values and virtues.

Not so much virtual working, more virtuous working

Not good value

Let's have a look at the sort of thing that usually passes muster as standard company values, the sort you find on the wall in company board rooms the world over. Oh boy, are these inspirational:

Continuous improvement
Openness and honesty
Availability and professionalism
Putting customers first
Respecting people
Embracing ideas and creativity
Non-hierarchical
Encouraging and helping
Focused but visionary
Network, partnership and community driven

If these are your company values, do they get you going? Do they, hell! They are boring, dull, unemotional, unimaginative, indistinctive, unliveable, and did I say dull? If I haven't already said it, get a life. If you don't think there is a problem here, let's have a look at a few of those so-called values.

Continuous improvement, what the hell does that mean? You can just see it can't you?

'Hi Rich, how are you?'

'Oh, hi Jacky, I'm really busy today, I'm doing continuous improvement.'

This is a classic corporate aspiration being passed off as a value.

Openness and honesty. You can't use things like this just as you can't in personal relationships. A guy goes up to a girl in a bar and says:

'Hey, my name's Martin and I'm open and honest.'

The open may go down OK but the honest is a no-no. Just so in corporate life. What about professionalism? We've already got dress down Friday, how about be professional Monday?

Continuous improvement, what the hell does that mean?

Most of the others are just as bad. Focused but visionary? I don't think so. Non-hierarchical, this is a cracker. There is this fantastic trend at the moment for flat organisations, which is great in principle; it keeps everyone close to the customer and close to the CEO. But in every company I've worked for it doesn't quite seem to work. Everyone is flat but some people are a lot flatter than others. You know the sort of thing. Everyone is going to lose their offices, except the boss, no more first-class flights, except the top grade. Everyone must share secretaries, except the top guys who have two secretaries and a PA.

Corporate values must be realistic. They must be applied to everyone, and they must prompt action. And that is the rub; most do not.

Move over old values. Like many old economy business practices, they are corporate dinosaurs and should be extinct.

Everyone is flat but some people are a lot flatter than others

So what exactly are values and virtues?

Values are the foundation of your organisation. They set the tone for how you work together as a team.

Virtues are your organisation's front door. They set the tone for the way you interact with customers.

Values are your internal drivers. Virtues are your external drivers.

Both values and virtues must tie in totally with your brand. Both must be measurable.

As an individual, your values are your beliefs, the things that motivate every action you take and every decision you make. Your value is your intrinsic worth, the determinant of your quality. Virtue is the practice of duty, the practice of excellent qualities. As an organisation, values and virtues apply in the same way to you.

New economy new values

What makes human economy values different to old values?

New values are directly connected to your brand.

New values should be distinctive, highly memorable, and inspirational to any member of your organisation.

New values must be liveable, and linked to a process for reviewing them both as individuals and the organisation as a whole.

New values should form part of the contract between the organisation and all employees.

Values should be focused around the critical few.

Welcome to Virtue Park

What makes a brand virtue and why do they work?

Virtues are integral to and derived from your brand.

Virtues must be as distinctive and appealing as any other aspect of your brand. A customer should be able to recognise you by your virtues alone.

Virtues must be liveable, and linked to a process for reviewing them both for individuals and the organisation as a whole.

Virtues should form part of the contract between the organisation and all employees.

Virtues should be focused around the critical few.

Living life

Is it easy to use?

Yes, the basics are very easy to understand. You can even do it as a person on your own to get an invaluable insight into your organisation. The real value of life, however, is when the whole company buys into it. Achieving that is where you need to be clever.

Link up to www.BrandStorm.com

Who can apply life?

You can use life as a quick 30 minute test of the brand spirit living in your people. When it really works however, is when it is an accepted contract by everyone in the organisation. To achieve that, you must involve the whole organisation in life, and the development of your values and virtues. If you can't walk it, don't talk it!

How can life be applied?

Life should be applied to the whole organisation responsible for a brand.

Life can be used as the basis of both one-to-one, personal reviews, and overall organisational performance reviews.

Does life review actual behaviour or aspiration?

Both. You should use life to set expected behaviour, and then use the life process to review performance against expectation.

If you can't walk it, don't talk it!

Step by step to life

Step one – Start communicating

Involve everyone in life as early as you can.

Step two – Choose your values and virtues

Choose values and virtues that are truly distinctive and capture the essence of your personality.

Step three – Illuminate your values and virtues

Create a story for each value and virtue that brings it alive.

Step four – Life review in action

Starting at the top, introduce personal life reviews for everyone in the organisation.

Step five – Life audit your organisation

Understand life in your organisation from the perspective of those who actually live it.

Step six – Start improving your life

Set improvement targets and use life to make your values and virtues real.

Values are for life,
not just
for
christmas

Getting a life

The core purpose of life is to make your brand live in your people and for your customers. It is not a standard review process and it is not about identifying generally useful interpersonal behaviours. If it is not on brand it shouldn't be in. It is not about uniformity or lack of individuality either.

Step one – Start communicating

Link up to www.BrandStorm.com

- **Life works for both values and virtues. Follow the same procedure for both. Start each step with your values and then your virtues.**

- **Ensure total top to bottom, left to right involvement.**

- **Instigate fantastic, straightforward, quality communication. Tell everyone what you are going to do, why, how, and when you are doing it. Then do it, and tell everyone what you have done.**

- **Use the people involved to communicate face to face with everyone in the company.**

Make sure that it is clear that life is owned and will be lived by your leader but don't think that on its own this will make a difference. It won't. People will have heard all that stuff before and seen ideas come and go till they are blue in the face: TQM, EQA, etc.

Be clear that life is not a change programme. Once agreed and contracted, values and virtues are for life, not just for Christmas. Well, maybe not quite for life, but they are the way you underwrite your brand. They are the foundation of your brand promise and customer expectation.

Step two — Choosing your values and virtues

■ Discover your values and virtues through a series of small and involving cascade workshops featuring every department, function, sector, and level in the company.

■ Make your workshops iterative so the first people involved see, and can review, the work coming out of the later workshops.

■ Use my description of the brand storm values and virtues as a catalyst to choosing yours.

What should your values and virtues contain? Well, I can't tell you that I'm afraid, but let's start by looking at your values. These need to be totally personal to you, in fact, they must fit you like a glove.

To get an idea of what to aim for, though, let's re-examine the *Brand Storm* values:

Openness
Fairness
Passion
Belief
Humanity
Hope

Why did we choose these values for *Brand Storm*?

To start with, we had to limit ourselves to six or it became an endless, and meaningless, wish list. Openness was critical to a book incorporating so many themes and ideas. If we weren't passionate about writing this book it would never have happened, and I don't mean that these applied just to me as the author. Without a passionate publishing and design team we would never have managed to challenge the traditional business book mould to produce *Brand Storm* in the way we have.

Your values must fit you like a glove

Fairness is key to the way *Brand Storm* has been put together, and belief has been critical from the start. Without humanity and hope we may well have started the book but never finished it.

Having values has held a physically dispersed team together. Everyone involved, from the front cover designer, through the web page designers to the photographers and dreamers, has approached their contribution to the book in the same spirit, producing, I hope, a much better reader experience as a result.

What about your virtues? There is no definitive answer but each set of virtues should be as unique to your organisation as your fingerprints are to you. Again, it is probably useful to use the *Brand Storm* virtues as a guide.

Having established the values for the team we created our virtues. These formed the framework for talking to our customers, which, in our case, determined the style of our book and website. These were the virtues we chose:

Insight
Imagination
Illumination
Inspiration
Ignition
Involvement

I guess the first thing to say is that not all virtues need to start with the letter 'i', in fact they don't need to start with the same anything. In our case, they just seemed to flow out all starting with the same letter. Why did we choose these virtues?

What use is any business-orientated book to a reader if it does not contain insight? We didn't want just to be insightful, though; we wanted to be imaginative in both what we said, and the way we said it. We also wanted to stir your imagination.

Each set of virtues should be as unique to your organisation as your fingerprints are to you

The next virtue has been instrumental to *Brand Storm*. Anyone can tell a story, we wanted to illuminate our ideas through words, pictures, design, and graphics. We wanted to join you in celebrating business. I guess that leads straight onto the next virtue, inspiration. This applies both to the book's style of presentation, and to the emotion that we are trying to create in you, the reader.

If we have not prompted and enabled you to take action already, then *Brand Storm* has failed in its real objective. This is where ignition came in.

Lastly, involvement. *Brand Storm* has been designed from inception as an interactive book. We want you to use the website in implementing *Brand Storm*. We want to talk to you and for you to talk to each other about your brand storming experiences. We want to talk to you about any experiences you have of customer love.

Step three – Illuminate your values and virtues

Link up to www.BrandStorm.com

- **Once you have chosen your values and virtues, create a ten-second message to capture the unique meaning of each value and virtue in the context of your organisation.**

Taking a *Brand Storm* example of a ten-second message, 'Collaboration' reads:

'*Brand Storm* is an open venture. If someone can help us project our virtues while sharing our values, welcome them.'

- **Follow this with a more detailed single side of paper on each value and virtue, containing examples of relevant applications in your organisation.**

- **Make sure that your expanded statements are agreed with by all those involved in the initial creation process.**

- **Communicate your values and virtues to the whole organisation.**

Your embryonic values and virtues won't, at this stage, be adding value to your organisation. Now is the time to inject them into the lifeblood of your organisation.

Step four – Life review in action

- Life review is a fantastically simple way to review people's behaviour and delivery against brand expectation. It uses a 360-degree performance review process for discussing and recording individual personal performance against your agreed values and virtues.

  Values are used to assess behaviour.

  Virtues are used to assess output.

- Introduce life review in a series of waves so that the introducing managers are operating the process themselves before they use it with people they manage.

- Individual life reviews should be conducted monthly between a manager and the people they manage, hopefully as part of existing mentoring and review processes.

- Both parties review each other's performance against values and virtues prior to the meeting, scoring each one out of four and preparing any supporting evidence

- One represents very poor, two below average, three good, and four excellent.

Here is an example using the brand storm values and virtues:

Values				
(Behaviour)	Score			
	1	2	3	4
Openness			*	
Fairness				*
Passion				*
Belief			*	
Humanity				*
Hope			*	
Virtues	1	2	3	4
(Output)				
Insight			*	
Imagination				*
Illumination				*
Inspiration			*	
Ignition			*	
Involvement		*		

- Meet and discuss how you both think you have performed, not forgetting this a totally democratic process providing upward and downward feedback. Both take notes for next month's review.

- Recognise and reward your top performers as seen from the team member as well as the manager perspective.

Loving by design

Not just your managers, not just your customer-facing staff, absolutely everyone must stand up and be counted when it comes to pulling together for your customers. When your values and virtues start to drive everything you think, and everything you do, you are on the right road.

- **Now is the time to start to think about building your values and virtues into the fabric of your organisation. With life review in place as a 360-degree review process, everybody from the chairman downwards, regardless of their function, should want to take shared responsibility for living your brand. Introduce value and virtue performance measures into your contracts of employment and remuneration packages as well as your recruitment advertising and procedures.**

Step five – Life audit your organisation

Having developed a system for reviewing individual performance against your values and virtues, the next stage is to consider overall performance.

- **Audit current perceptions of performance against your values and virtues every six to 12 months. Respondents should be asked for their view of how every key audience group is performing against each value and virtue.**

Example questions:

How well does the organisation's senior management apply our values and virtues?

How well does your immediate management apply our values and virtues?

How well do your peers apply our values and virtues?

How well does any specific group, division or department perform (e.g. sales, customer service etc.)?

Values		Score			
(Behaviour)		1	2	3	4
Openness			*		
Fairness				*	
Passion					*
Belief			*		
Humanity					*
Hope				*	
Virtues		1	2	3	4
(Output)					
Insight				*	
Imagination				*	
Illumination					*
Inspiration				*	
Ignition				*	
Involvement			*		

■   To obtain unbiased results, and establish benchmarks and departmental comparisons, returns should be recorded down to department level but not be assignable to specific individuals.

Link up to www.BrandStorm.com

■   When you have conducted your life audit you can add up all your scores and work out your net performance figures. You will have enough information to look at the dynamics of how your organisation is performing. You can cut the information by function, by department or by division. In fact, you can cut the information any which way.

Step six – Start improving your life

■ **Now is the time to start using your information to drive your organisation forward. Always reward good behaviour, do not penalise bad or life will become an unpleasant chore.**

■ **Set improvement targets for every group in the organisation.**

■ **Re-audit in six months' time.**

Remember, you are not alone. Go to the website and let us know how you are getting on with the implementing of life. Share your ideas. Share your successes.

Why does life work?

It forms an agreed contract between all employees.

It cuts out non-productive behaviour and focuses on brand goals.

It is non-hierarchical and 360-degree applicable.

Life's measurable criteria make reviews non-contentious, and non-judgmental, and can sit alongside existing appraisal and review processes.

Progress can be audited company wide.

Life can be applied to supplier, customer, and recruitment relationships.

It is easy to live, understand, and communicate.

SNAPSHOT

Any time your whole organisation isn't living your brand, you're losing customers.

Create a work sensation.

Buy people not parts.

Wear the shoes you want filled.

Stand or fall by your values.

Be virtuous in your customers' eyes.

Unite your whole organisation on a single crusade or blow in the wind.

KICKER:

Life Immerses your people in your brand.

Force

Force is the last of the *Brand Storm* diagnostics and builds on takes one, two, and three. If you have already applied the ideas in those takes, you will have unified your ideas, actions and brands, put your customers and brands at the heart of your organisation, and started to immerse your customers in a living brand. 'Force' takes it one stage further, breaking down functional barriers both within your organisation, and across your extended enterprise and partner network.

Problem children

When you see what is euphemistically called a 'problem child', many people will say, 'You know the problem there, it is not the kid, it's the parents.' In a lot of cases, they are right.

And when you think about it, there are a lot of similarities between organisations and small children. They both need a great deal of attention, are expensive to keep, eat up a lot of your time, and are prone to throwing their weight around. In fact, the list is endless.

As is also the case with children, problems start for many organisations before the organisations are even born. The moment a person starts to think about an opportunity, preconceptions and personal bias start to take hold. By the time the organisation is actually born, the scene is set for the parents' insecurities and peccadilloes to take a hold in the new-born organisation.

For an organisation, this means an undue focus on one aspect of the business, be it the product, technology, or finance. Not only do these areas dominate management time, they also set a pattern of functional dominance, and, worst of all, lead to silo-based organisational structures.

Organisations are like small children; they both make a lot of mess for you to clear up

Meet the family

If things get off to a bad start with the parents, for your average organisation, worse is still to come. Meet the family.

So to whom am I referring as the family? Well, to start with there are partners, shareholders, trade unions, and investors. Now we are really starting to confuse the child. Important strategic issues and major aspects of the organisation are agreed, not with the organisation's best interests at heart, but to meet the requirements of immediate stakeholders. Revenue targets, payback periods, staff levels, office locations, the organisation's name, partnerships, routes to market, key appointments and non-execs all start to get decided on to meet the varied and often conflicting agendas of the family.

Unfortunately, as we live in the real world, an element of this cannot be avoided. The most damaging result, however, is on an organisation's board of directors.

Interest-driven appointments cause conflict, create vision and value fuzziness, and organisation-wide virtues get killed off at birth.

At worst, this can lead to corporate schizophrenia, and commonly it propagates organisational sectarianism and antagonistic functional silos. The brand stops being everyone's key purpose and responsibility and becomes the domain of marketing. Walls get built up between departments, personal battles rage, communication and working together goes to pot.

And it gets worse. There is the extended family. Interest groups, government, regulators, industry associations, and even inward investment groups. All these groups will foster division in the organisation, and deepen functional interests and organisational silos.

If you think the parents are bad meet the whole family

Welcome to adolescence

Having successfully navigated childhood, the growing organisation marches on to puberty. Not a pretty sight. Spots, raging hormones, rapidly changing voice and appearance, bits growing all over the place, body parts doing things they never used to, new friends, new challenges – and new pitfalls. Charm and communication go out the window, replaced by sulkiness and the opposite sex.

In organisational terms, this means growing pains. Alternative strategies rear their head: takeovers and mergers become a live issue. E-mails and one-to-ones are the order of the day. Why talk to someone if an e-mail will do? Everyone is busy, busy, busy.

And what is the best solution for a sulky disrespectful teenager with more money than sense? You've guessed it, therapy. And so with organisations, only they don't call it therapy, they call it consultancy. It's change team time.

No replays

I could go on to mid-life crisis and old age but you are probably getting the picture by now. Organisations, like people, develop a life of their own and it's a messy, confused life. Again, like people, there are times in their life when organisations need to stop, take stock, and take a long hard look at how they are living their life. What they are spending their time doing, who are their friends, and are they achieving the goals they want to achieve in a way they are happy to do so? This isn't a rehearsal, it's life.

Most companies are naturally too product, shareholder, or even, in some cases of organisations without their own vision, too customer led to develop their own balanced psyche. The older they become the more set in their ways they become. They create a clan culture with staff loyalty to colleagues not the company psyche, thereby encouraging conflicts of interest.

This is extremely common today and not limited to large or established companies. I have seen small companies with 20 staff or less, split into very distinct clans, hardly talking to each other and never socialising.

Corporate adolescence is not a pretty sight. Bits growing all over the place, body parts doing things they never used to

Stress fractures

Some modern working practices are exacerbating this as well. Virtual working, hot-desking, etc, allow a new level of freedom for people, but are creating a growing disassociation with their employer. People may feel part of a team, but not of the organisation. This can be very dangerous for the overall performance of the organisation, and needs to be countered.

Many companies expect cross-team, cross-functional co-operation to just happen, doing nothing to encourage it. The reality being, however, that many of today's processes and systems actually create barriers to co-operation.

Good ideas are not harvested from the customer interface, customer-facing staff are not listened to enough, even when they can generate solutions that benefit the whole organisation.

Most of today's corporate value chains extend beyond the barriers of the organisation to suppliers, partners, and even customers. As we said earlier, no organisation is an island, and changes at one end of a logistics chain can bring enormous benefits to other parts of the chain. The benefits of customers directly accessing supplier information, and vice versa, are well proven. This type of close co-operation also encourages loyalty and can pre-empt problems.

Come together

Market forces are making continuous change a way of life, which is great, and how it should be. The challenge that it throws up, though, is to maintain fantastic service through continuous organisational disruption. There will be endless opportunities to drop the ball, endless diversions, and endless job insecurities getting in the way of serving your customers. Have you ever tried juggling while driving round a car park looking for a space? Give it a try. See how it feels.

All of this throws up the need for a radical rethink of the whole subject of organisational structures to support total flexibility and rapid action but still cater for the fact that your employees are all human, not superman, and suffer the same understandable insecurities as you do. Quite a challenge.

Part of the answer will be co-operating jointly with your partners to support the natural 'virtual communities' that flow in and out of your organisation, while at the same time using your values as a kernel to build your organisation around.

—— Have you ever tried juggling while driving round a car park looking for a parking space?

Purpose driven

Organisations that use their brand vision, brand values, and brand virtues to drive their communications, their people, and their value chains will have integrity in all they do. These are the organisations that will start to perfect cross-functional co-operation. They will become less silo driven, more purpose driven, and far more resilient to the ravages of continual change. Individuals will start to draw their sense of self-esteem and self-worth not from their position within an artificially rigid organisation, but from their identifiable and recognised contribution to an evolving value chain.

Not only will these organisations work better and be far less stressful to work for, they will be better connected to their environment, making them less vulnerable to unforeseen change. At the end of the day, these organisations will add far more value to all their stakeholders. Enabling this is where force comes in.

What is force?

Years of working in large companies have left me amazed and rather depressed at the waste and prevarication that goes on. I have consistently encountered people doing the most stupid things to win departmental arguments. Managers who care more about their budget than their customers and who, at the end of a financial year, will spend money on anything rather than risk losing some of their budget the following year. Managers filling any headcount they can lay their hands on to make their department bigger. Managers who will do or say just about anything to keep their job. And talk about dull. Everyone has the right to be dull but some of these guys abuse it.

I now believe that if you drive organisations forward functionally you shoot your customer service in the foot, while wasting money hand over fist. You tie a lead weight around the ankle of change, and blindfold innovation. It might be the right approach for a brothel, but it's no way to run a business. Force creates communities that are driven by your vision, values, and virtues. They are focused not around traditional functions with organisational boundaries but on the value chains that flow in and out of your organisation. Value chains that flow in from your suppliers and partners, and out to your downstream partners and customers.

Force promotes non-hierarchical value chain champions and recognises the contribution of anyone who makes even the smallest contribution to the success of the chain. It is measurable, visual, cuts through crap, and is fun to be part of.

Why use force?

Force liberates people from their functional shackles.

Force gathers ideas from everybody involved in your brand value chains and fosters the development of best practice.

Force creates real commitment to achieving your psyche.

Force protects customer service levels even through periods of disruption.

Force drives knowledge management by creating natural communities of interest.

Force crosses international boundaries.

Force supports market sector focus, virtual and matrix working.

Force brings suppliers, partners, and customers into the organisation.

Functional management ties a leadweight around change, and blindfolds innovation.
It might be the right approach for a brothel, but it's no way to run a business

May the force be with you

Is it easy to use?

Yes, the basics are very easy to understand, and every step is supported by the brand storm website. Even as an individual, you can obtain an invaluable insight into your organisation using force. The real value of force, however, is when it is bought into and operated by the whole company. To achieve this is a greater but fulfilling challenge.

Link up to www.BrandStorm.com

Who can apply force?

Anyone can be the catalyst for getting force working in your organisation. How strong is your will? It is perfectly reasonable for several links in an extended value chain to implement force at the same time, and you can belong to more than one community simultaneously.

How can force be applied?

Force should be applied to all the contributors, and to your key value chains, regardless of whether they are part of your organisation or not. Invite others in, be a leader, not a lagger.

Does force review actual behaviour or aspiration?

Both. You should use force to set expectation, then use brand marking to review performance.

Be a leader, not a lagger

Step by step to force

Step one – Start communicating

Involve everyone in force as early as you can.

Step two – Identify your value chains

Identify the most important value chains that run through your organisation.

Step three – Illuminate your value chains

Describe each value chain and bring them alive.

Step four – Introduce brand marking

Score the perception of how well each of your value chains is working.

Step five – Review your whole organisation

Identify all the audience groups who took part and compare the pictures they paint.

Step six – Start being forceful

Create your value chain communities and start the serious task of improving performance.

Step one – Start communicating

The first thing to think about, as with the rest of *Brand Storm* is communication. You want total involvement, so communicate early, communicate well, and never make anything a fait accompli.

Link up to www.BrandStorm.com

■ Contact the key individuals across your own organisation, partners, suppliers, and customers, who should be involved. Explain to them what you are doing, and why the force process is important. If you are implementing other parts of *Brand Storm* put force in the context of other things you are doing. When you are involving people from outside your own organisation, your initial approach will be very important to your success. If you get it right, they will be flattered that you need their involvement, and usually very supportive.

■ Think about how you are going to get people together to work on this, and, for God's sake, make it fun. Who wants another dreary awayday? With representatives present from your whole organisation, suppliers, partners, and customers, let your hair down, and do some bonding. It's great for building up loyalty. Just because something is serious doesn't mean it can't be fun.

Step two – Identify your value chains

Your actual value chains will be specific to your organisation but to kick the process off, some generic value chains that apply to most companies follow.

■ Use these to start a debate with your chosen players, and adjust them to fit your priorities. When identifying your value chains stick to a maximum of ten, otherwise it is hard to manage the process with everything becoming a value chain. If you can get away with fewer, do so.

■ Let people be creative, go below the surface, and find out exactly how business actually gets done.

For God's sake, make it fun. Who wants another dreary awayday?

Example value chains

Creating business strategy

Is creating strategy quick, funky, and wired?

Are your strategy documents visually engaging?

Do you ask your friends for feedback?

Do you involve your whole organisation, supplies, partners, and customers?

Is your strategy in tune with your wishbone?

Does it lead your marketing and planning processes?

Managing people

Is your HR policy an open book to employees, customers, and partners?

Do your values and virtues drive your HR policy?

When was the last time a HR person won a sales or marketing award?

Do you bring customer-facing staff into HR jobs?

Does the whole company work together to recruit the best new staff?

Is HR everyone's job, and do you help everyone do it?

Developing new products and services

Does everyone get involved with developing new products and services?

Do you quickly pick up and action ideas from everywhere?

Are your products and services virtue led?

When was the last time HR won a sales award?

The sales process

Does selling stop and start with your sales force or is everyone a salesman?

Are sales and marketing joined at the hip?

Do your senior managers know how to sell?

Are you networking as standard?

Does your selling approach ooze your values and virtues?

Your marketing programmes

Is marketing everyone's job?

Does everyone live the brand?

Do you reward the whole organisation against your brand's performance?

Advertising and communicating

If you want to communicate, do you start with your own people?

Do all your people love your advertising?

Do your advertising and communication people walk the same talk?

Are your partners involved in your communication?

Serving customers

Does everyone in your company revere your customer-facing staff?

Does everyone know what a tough job this is?

Does everyone help to make it easier?

Do your customer servers feel loved?

Are sales and marketing joined at the hip?

Managing knowledge

Is managing knowledge a natural act?

Does everyone access and contribute to your knowledge bank? Indeed, is everyone allowed to, encouraged to, rewarded to, and do they want to?

Is knowledge the heart of your organisation?

Buying, distributing, and handling stock

Is managing stock an enterprise-wide role, seamless from buyer to customer?

Do your suppliers and customers trust you?

Do you share each other's problems, and want to help?

Managing profit

Is everyone responsible for profit?

Do you reward everyone for greater profit?

Does everyone know the facts?

Do your finance guys understand your customers?

Is managing knowledge a natural act?

Step three – Illuminate your value chains

Link up to www.BrandStorm.com

- Once you have agreed on your value chains, write a brief description of each.

Step four – Introduce brand marking

- As with any brand storm model, measurement is pivotal. To provide an organisational x-ray, and a base point for improvement plans and improvement targets, conduct a brand marking exercise.

- Brand marking works by asking as many people as possible in your extended enterprise their views on how well each of your value chains is working. If you want to know what is going on, ask those doing it.

- Create a standard pro forma listing all your value chains with supporting descriptions. Ask each person to score his or her perception of the performance of each value chain from one to four. Provide any supporting data that may be useful.

One = Poor
Needs urgent attention.

Two = Below best competitors
You should be better than all your competitors at everything. If you are not, you need to know where your weak links are. If you have information on your competitor's methods and industry standards, share it.

Three = Great
Some reason to be proud of these processes.

Four = World class
Focus on these, your competitors will be copying you. To be world class means not just being the best in your field, but being as good or better at this than any organisation in the world.

If you want to know what is going on, ask those doing it

Here is an example, using the value chains introduced earlier, that has been scored:

Value Chain	Scores			
	1	**2**	**3**	**4**
Business strategy		*		
Managing people				*
New products and services			*	
The sales process		*		
Marketing	*			
Advertising	*			
Serving customers		*		
Managing knowledge				*
Buying and distributing stock			*	
Managing profit		*		

- ■ In order to obtain unbiased results so that you can establish benchmarks and departmental comparisons, returns should be recorded down to department or partner/customer level, but not be assignable to specific individuals.

- ■ Once you have conducted your brand marking exercise you can get a top line view on how your organisation is performing.

Link up to www.BrandStorm.com

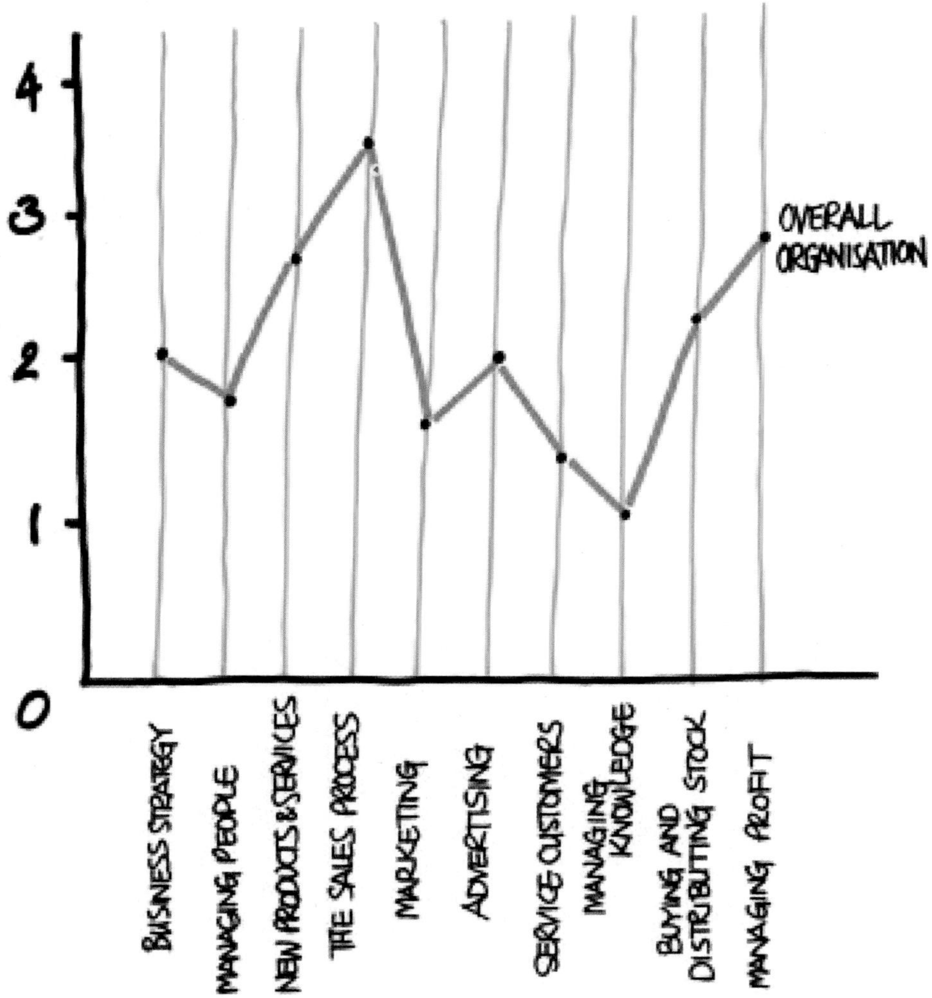
4
3
2
1
0
OVERALL ORGANISATION
BUSINESS STRATEGY
MANAGING PEOPLE
NEW PRODUCTS & SERVICES
THE SALES PROCESS
MARKETING
ADVERTISING
SERVICE CUSTOMERS
MANAGING KNOWLEDGE
BUYING AND DISTRIBUTING STOCK
MANAGING PROFIT

Create your own force profiles

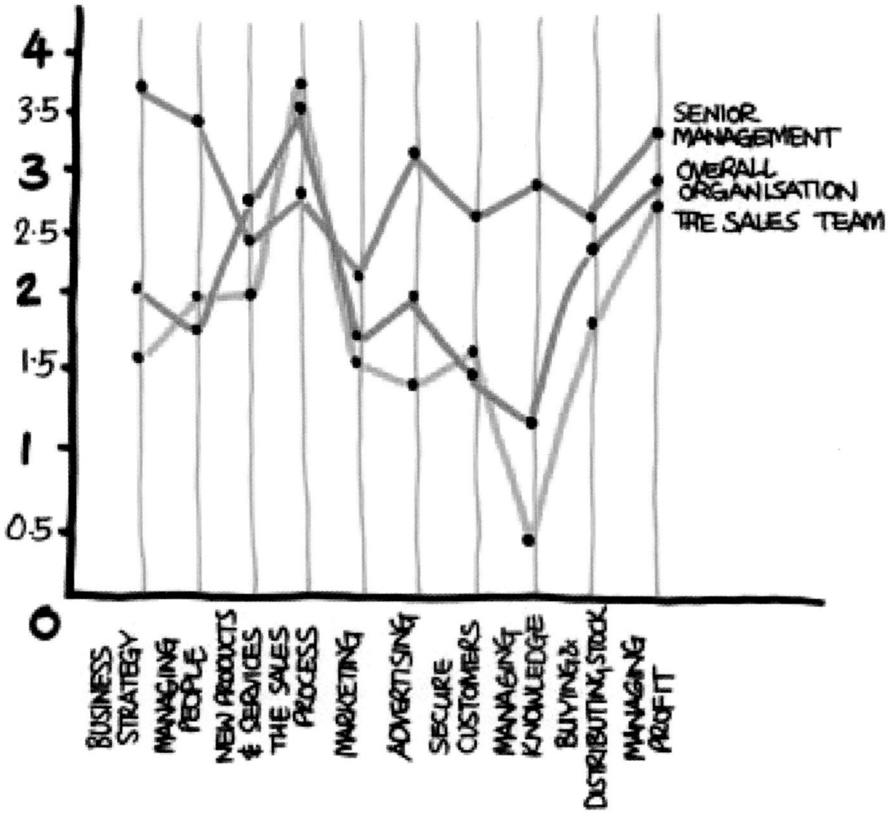
4
3.5
3
2.5
2
1.5
1
0.5
0
SENIOR MANAGEMENT
OVERALL ORGANISATION
THE SALES TEAM
BUSINESS STRATEGY
MANAGING PEOPLE
NEW PRODUCTS & SERVICES
THE SALES PROCESS
MARKETING
ADVERTISING
SECURE CUSTOMERS
MANAGING KNOWLEDGE
BUYING & DISTRIBUTING STOCK
MANAGING PROFIT

Step five – Review your whole organisation

- Once you have your top line profile input, you have the information for each of your key audience groups. Typical groups would be: Market sector teams. Different divisions. Different functions. Senior management. Partners who took part. A value chain community.
- Create and compare the profiles of your different groups. Do they follow the same trend or show marked differences? Who thinks you are performing the best, and who thinks performance is poor?

Step six – Start being forceful

■ You will quickly see where your problems are, and where your strengths lie. Pull together the team you used at the start of the process and review your results. Make sure you provide immediate feedback to all those who were involved in the brand marking audit.

■ Prioritise which of your value chains would benefit from extra attention and build value chain improvement teams around these. I would suggest that you limit yourself to a maximum of three or four.

■ Physically get your value chain teams together, infuse them with your excitement, and appoint value chain champions. In choosing your champions pick well-respected, natural leaders with a genuine interest in the area in question, but steer clear of those with direct functional responsibility unless there is a compelling reason to choose them.

■ Your new communities can now start the serious task of improving performance. Set targets for improvement so you can re-brand mark in six or 12 months, and review your progress.

Only organisations living in extended communities can prosper in the human economy.

Harvest every idea.

Avoid a clan culture.

Let your partners live your virtues.

Protect your customer experience.

Be inclusive not exclusive.

Think value not function; liberate people from their corporate shackles.

Force lets you operate without boundaries.

Scene three

DREAMS

Daring to dream, and dreaming to dare

The first two *Brand Storm* scenes are designed to inspire and ignite action. The purpose of 'Dreams' is a little different.

'Dreams' is about daring to dream, and daring to be different. 'Dreams' is designed to add tone and texture to the *Brand Storm* experience. My initial brief to potential dreamers was simple but vague:

'Taking the Internet as a catalyst, and exploring the importance of mutual trust, respect, and admiration in the human economy, I am writing a book called *Brand Storm*. The intention is to inspire people to create, and pursue, their own dreams in this new Internet-inspired but human-orientated world'.

'Do you have a dream that inspires you, and that you would like to share?'

What I didn't want was lots of moody shots of self-satisfied CEOs trying to look charismatic and mysterious, while at the same pumping out jargon and corporate speak, peppered with references to last year's well-known brands.

I sent the brief out to all sorts of people, some well known some not, some corporate leaders and again some not. The initial response was universally positive until push came to shove and people realised that what was required was a personal dream laced with their own passion and beliefs, not just distilled wisdom delivered from up high.

This sorted out the men from the boys. If this little test is anything to go by, it proves that the bigger the company you work for, and the more senior your role, the less passionate you become, and the less you dream.

Every dream here has inspired me, and every dream is different. I didn't plan it this way but the dreams seem to fall roughly into three categories. Those concerned with seizing new opportunities, those that revel in the democratic effect of the human economy, and those that celebrate new dimensions and perspectives in thinking liberated by the diversity, speed, and spirit of the human economy. I have made no attempt to sift the dreams into any specific order, but instead have tried to create a garden of discovery with a surprise around every corner.

Every dreamer here has already started to embrace the spirit of the human economy. I hope that 'Dreams' inspires you to become a brand storm pioneer.

Job title and company:
Corporate Services Manager, Cyberia

Description of job:
Internet consultant and strategist

Contact details:
rleader@easynet.co.uk
www.theinternetcompany.co.uk

What are you most proud of?
Cooking a 7 course dinner party for 8 guests on a Baby Belling when one of the rings didn't work if you had the grill on.

What do you remember most from your childhood?
Wanting to be a DJ – sitting on my best friend's bedroom floor with a turntable, a mike, speakers, loads of cables and a stack of Shakin' Stevens LPs. I live in permanent fear that someone will one day discover the tapes we made.

Who is your hero?
I ought to say Tim Berners-Lee, but probably the late George Hall – lecturer in Theology at St. Andrews University – a great man, massively intelligent, creative and humane (and a great storyteller).

Where is your favourite place in the world? My bed on a Saturday morning with a cup of tea and a fag (cigarette for US readers).

Have you ever been in love and what did it feel like?
I thought I was in love throughout my poetry-writing teenage years and it felt awful – not dissimilar to the stomach-bug I picked up last time I was on holiday. Now I know it to create a warm, contented feeling, a bit like whisky.

What do you still want to achieve?
Either to run a Michelin-starred restaurant or to be Rex Bob Lowenstien.

RICHARD LEADER

Who is to say what is for the best?

Richard Leader – an innovative vision

Innovate v. introduce (changes, new things)

Vision n. 1 sight 2 insight 3 dream 4 phantom 5 imagination

Dream n. 1 vision during sleep 2 fancy 3 reverie 4 aspiration 5 very pleasant idea, person, thing

Technology n. 1 application of practical, mechanical sciences to industry, commerce 2 technical methods, skills, knowledge

Genuine, innovative, visionary technological advances in the field of communication do not exist at present because we are locked into a narrow and constricted view of what communication is. We are hampered by our context, and unable to break out of our old world view to seize the new culture of extreme science. Today's science is about minuscule technology and massive ideas. Technology should be about the cellular, not the mechanical. Our view of communication is currently mechanical, old world, industrialist and embedded in thousands of years of cumulative context and experience.

To look at the future of anything, however, we still need to be aware of its context. To look at the future of communication technology, we need to ask ourselves what the prevailing media are at the moment. They are the tv, radio, newspapers, telephones, fax machines, e-mail, books, magazines, teachers, the WWW, junk mail, SMS messages, conversations in the pub. They are all pretty much the same, though, and little has changed for thousands of years.

For example, a newspaper is a means of transmitting information and opinion to a large, distinct group of individuals for the purposes of edification, usually created for profit (financial, political or idealistic). A newspaper is a more technically proficient smoke signal. It is the more modern church sermon.

A satellite tv news broadcast is a more technically proficient newspaper. Even the communication structure is the same – a group of linear stories introduced by headlines (teasers to catch our interest), and journalists bringing their opinions, their versions of stories, to a mass audience. The fact that it happens live (as opposed to the newspaper bringing us yesterday's stories) makes it more like the smoke signal than the newspaper is. The fact that it is bounced between pieces of technical equipment until it reaches the tv in your hotel room makes it more like the tribal drums used across the vast territories of Africa – one village relaying the story to the next.

Having pictures of the event does not make the communication mechanism any different. Indeed, plenty of blind people tune in to the tv news every evening. Plenty of blind people have newspapers read to them or use Braille or the Internet; the pictures generally add nothing to the story – the story is the same as it was before the invention of photography.

My point is that most innovation in this field is aimed at making the actual act of communicating quicker, more efficient and wider reaching, but not necessarily better or different. It is about perfecting the current product, and not about looking for a new vision.

Innovations in mobile telephony mean we are better able to contact the outside world wherever we are. The means of communication is still the same: a voice-based conversation, an e-mail or a WAP site are all just ways of transmitting information and opinions using words. We still learn by assimilating information verbally or visually. The only difference now is that we have far more access to a global sea of information and experience. However, it is the same conversation as before; it's just a bit easier, quicker, and more efficient. We are better able to tap into libraries of information, but the libraries themselves are the same as the great Library of Alexandria. The storage mechanism and the access might be different, but the theory is the same. Indeed, the Dublin Core index system some people are working on to index the web is based on the old library Dewey system. This time, however, we do not need to live in Alexandria to access the library. The library itself has a global reach because of technology.

Genuine transformation of our condition through innovation will take place at the cellular or subcellular organic level, probably through some form of genetic engineering. Only when we can implant a virus in someone's body, such as in Geoff Ryman's excellent novel *The Child Garden*, will we be able to stop the old world laborious process of learning through words and pictures. In Ryman's book, the virus automatically teaches us what we need to know about a particular subject and shapes our behaviour accordingly. In *The Matrix*, which surely learned much from *The Child Garden*, Neo learns from computer programs jammed into his brain. It is only when this sort of organic rather than mechanistic technology is available to us that anything will actually change.

Who is to say what is for the best?

At the start of the industrial age, who would have entertained the thought that we could produce so much, so small, so cheaply? At the beginning of this new 'information age', what can we say to stop people combining industrial-style technology with the very stuff of information, genetics? Only when we have the organic computer, the organic learning processes, the viral virtual reality, will we be able to say that we have progressed beyond the PC, the telephone, the WWW and the newspaper. Only when we have successfully changed the context for learning, the delivery and acceptance mechanisms will we have truly advanced. Then our whole context will have changed. History will still be there; indeed we can all know all about all history if we have the right virus. We won't need to learn any more, we won't need much of the communication that we currently use. We will all be able to devote our time to innovation, vision, dreams and technology.

But who is to say that it is for the best?

Job title and company:
Director – CEDAR International

Description of job: Coach

Contact details:
0207-496-9606 or 0370-853184

What are you most proud of?
My kids (Natalie and Daniel)

What do you remember most from your childhood?
My trike – motorbikes are still in my blood...

Who is your hero?
Anyone who 'just does it'.

Where is your favourite place in the world?
Devon if it's dry – Bali if it's not.

Have you ever been in love and what did it feel like? It felt like T.

What do you still want to achieve?
Autonomy!

NICK ELLSE

Want to join us?

The chairman's report

Today
"Employees are our most important asset."
[We tell them what to do.]

Tomorrow
"It's tough out there. Staff retention is down and customer satisfaction is failing. We have a plan..."
[Help.]

The Dream
"We listened to our customers and we listened to our people.
And we have done something about it. We look at individual needs
and support individuals in developing their capabilities and their
careers. And hey...customer loyalty is up...people want to join us
and our leavers are ambassadors for what we do."

Job title and company:
Chairman, eB2B Plc

Description of job:
Executive Chairman dealing with issues of strategy, investor relations and the impact of the new world of e-commerce.

Contact details:
eB2B PLC, 105 Piccadilly, London W1V 9FN Tel: 0207.6290201

What are you most proud of? Being able to laugh at myself when I screw up (which happens regularly).

What do you remember most from your childhood? As an only child, being totally spoilt by all the females in my family.

Who is your hero? Michael Winner for his dry sense of humour and outspoken believe in traditional standards of excellence.

Where is your favourite place in the world? Table Mountain in Cape Town – the rich colours, smells and sense of history are mind-blowing.

Have you ever been in love and what did it feel like? Exciting at the time – hell afterwards but I wouldn't have missed it for anything.

What do you still want to achieve? Find some way of materially contributing to the social balance sheet every day, rather than just the financial one.

RICHARD JAMES

Can you reach out and touch?

From here to ... affinity

As man moved from his accustomed role as a hunter–gatherer towards the new and stressful environment of the urban jungle, he lost his tribal affinity. Neither the Roman Catholic Church nor Manchester United Football Club has managed completely to fill this gap in modern man's need to identify with others. We desperately search around to brand ourselves, and send out messages to tell the world which tribe we belong to.

Walking to work this morning through South Kensington, I followed a smartly dressed couple for a few minutes. Nothing to distinguish them particularly: both typical denizens of South Kensington in their thirties, the man in a suit and the woman dressed modestly, as though they were both on their way to work. However, I couldn't help but notice that the woman had a small Louis Vuitton bag over her shoulder. This was her message to the world, and no doubt she had paid handsomely for it. We can work out what the Louis Vuitton bag was saying, but how does the advent of the Internet change the way we use the meta-tags of branding to communicate? Does it mean a better way of establishing the lost tribal affinity of man's former existence? I think it does: I call it 'tribal click'.

Just as tribes all over the world used the drum to communicate their messages, now the beat echoes through cyberspace as mouse-clicks. New virtual tribes form, broadcast their views, and interact with other tribes in the constantly evolving socio-economic primordial soup that is the WWW. (I like to call it 'the Cloud', perhaps because this conjures up the image of a wise old god sitting up there watching it all happen with some amusement.)

Connecting to the Cloud has empowered us all – we have access to the virtual world, with no borders, no limits, no pack drill, and no worries. That is, until someone starts messing with our virtual activities. Of course, there are the baddies lurking out there, and what better than a new untamed frontier for the greedy, unscrupulous, and perverted to operate in? The very freedom that allows the new tribes to form and communicate, perversely creates the conditions for many antisocial activities to flourish. So how do we tell the goodies from the baddies? Well, that's a hard one, but maybe it has something to do again with the concept of branding and tribal affinity. There will have to evolve some way of validating the value sets of those we communicate with.

We will adopt a virtual shadow, our personal persona in the Cloud – able to talk to all the other personas, affinity groups, organisations and corporations, and to act as the infomediary, making sure the baddies never get a look in.

Our shadow should have some human qualities, rather than being a glorified search engine for the cheapest, last-minute deal. It should be able to look around, talk to others, and tell us what our tribe can do to change the world for the better – especially the real world, where there will continue to be a majority of mankind living in comparative poverty for the foreseeable future. Perhaps helping those with no personal access to the Cloud and identifying with a compassionate tribe will become a more powerful message, producing greater satisfaction than a collection of expensive plastic handbags – this is my dream for the future of branding. It can be accomplished only if we can empower e-relationships with the ability to discriminate and personalise communication – that's a means to recall our lost tribal identities and reach out and touch those we want to influence, help, and interact with.

Job title and company:
Cultural Ambassador of Republic of Slovenia

Description of job:
I am a concert violinist and cultural entrepreneur.

Contact details:
mihaidriart@ibm.net

What are you most proud of?
Being *unemployed* all my life but feeling that in some way I am changing the world. But feeling that there is so much to do is like being on a small boat in the middle of the ocean.

What do you remember most from your childhood?
The smell of snow around our house in Slovenia.

Who is your hero?
Karl Ballmer, who unlocked for me the "who" dimension of Rudolf Steiner.

Where is your favourite place in the world?
Being amongst real friends anywhere.

Have you ever been in love and what did it feel like?
I am in love with my wife, love not given but regained.

What do you still want to achieve?
To learn better how to let the world manifest himself through my work. The first part of life is an illusion, in the second you start to integrate with the world.

MIHA POGACNIK

Do you remember the future?

Beginning knowledge

If you are charting your course through the rough waters of a mid-life crisis, you have probably experienced 'zero point' with walls everywhere. You wonder how you will ever break through to the next level. Then you remember what you have lost, perhaps in your youth: the Big Picture. Suddenly, this propels us to the next daring impossible.

In the fugue, a form of musical masterpiece, you hear the end in the first statement, and then the process starts evolving towards its glorious beginning. Just like the Creator becoming, in time, what he or she always is in presence: eternity.

Are you confused? Then that's a good start, because through contradictions we might come closer to the essence.

Let us look at the musical footprints in the picture. At the outset, you find a very strict introduction of the subject at different levels that don't tolerate any questioning. This can go on for a while but, eventually, this style drives a course towards chaos, to the inner frustration of command. After all, something can only grow for a certain time until it turns into a cancer. That triggers fear at the top, and commanders (the board) fire more of the same with more power, cascading the distorted subject to its own inner death. This oppressive cycle can be repeated many times, depending on budget and mindset.

But not in the musical masterpiece. In this case, once is enough. The same subject, but with a new beginning, and at another altitude, forms a canon. We hear conversation now, not dictation. The music is searching for heights and depths. If we are not attentive, we overhear the threshold to the next detour, away from the subject. As always, we want to go in one direction, but life gently pushes us in another. We agonise and complain, but introspection confirms that this detour was the best thing that could happen to us. So, here we are in the middle of an emerging future, musically unfolding into our experience. Masterpieces unfold meanings. In the light of the general crisis of meaning of modern day culture, it is healing to educate our fantasy with such processes. Gently oscillating its course at first, like resounding breath, music draws us with gravity to the very significant turmoil of archetypal human biography: the world education of mid-life crisis at the bottom of the drawing, a volcano erupting its Kundalini fire.

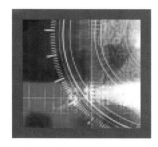

Dare to go through the fire without burning up? Or do we opt for illusionary security and become inner pensionists? This is the narrow path that we call 'centring'. We hear it as a roaring bass pedal tone. Foundations resound in the fire; fire is our element. Daring impossible is the meaning of life. Music goes on. Emerging on the other side, we live to tell the story. Where? Who? Remember the future!

After this long detour, the subject of origin and end is reintroduced. By concluding this section of the fugue, we are lifted to the next level. We thought we were already there, but real life is only just beginning. Now the subject is reintroduced upside down in the major mood, gently growing up.

Remember the first touch of hands with your first love? Who dares inwardness in our tough culture? But now in the corporate world, what used to be soft is becoming hard and central: sensitivity, flexibility, creativity, inspiration, even love for fellow human beings.

Finding in the fugue this gentle, upward, radiant quality is not the end. Rather, it is a discovery of inner substance (yes, leadership with substance!) that will mobilise us towards the final stages of archetypal biography: integration. We hear all elements experienced so far masterfully condensed as one, the music roaring to its completion of end and beginning.

Just before the end, the subject turns into a musical question. Who is asking whom about the tool we can't escape unless we sleep, the tool that begins any knowledge, and begins the knowledge about knowledge?

Can you imagine a world with no 'isms'

Job title and company:
CEO, VOODOO

Description of job:
Leadership and Vision

Contact details:
rene@voodoo-v.com 07831 166083

What are you most proud of?
My two children

What do you remember most from your childhood?
Burning ambition, hard work, tough environments, being black in a harsh white world.

Who is your hero?
Muhammad Ali. What he stood for, which was something different to everybody who saw or heard him.

Where is your favourite place in the world?
Florence/Tuscany

Have you ever been in love and what did it feel like?
It is thrilling and exhilarating but somehow never feeling totally sustainable.

What do you still want to achieve?
Sustained fun and friendships with like-minded people doing what we choose, where we choose.

RENÉ CARAYOL

Can you imagine a world with no 'isms'?

Diversity

The connected e-world of the 21st century presents us all with an unprecedented opportunity. Such a sentence is usually a preface to a barely disguised advertisement of some groundbreaking technology, or an uncannily comprehensive methodology. In other words, the 21st century has begun in the same pornographic flush of excitement as we ended the 20th, and 'unprecedented opportunity' means one thing: money. How much, and how quickly, can we all make some e-money? Just a couple of years ago, the big question used to be: Does anyone know anyone who is making money from the web? Now the question is: How can we catch up with those who appear to be on the point of making unimaginable sums of money on the web?

But what if there was something else to the Internet beyond money? What if this conjunction of technical possibility with human imagination and ingenuity was happening for some reason other than simply to give us all alternative routes of trade and sources of revenue?

The Internet has no 'isms'. Anybody who has access to the Internet can communicate and compete today. The web has no geographic barriers. We're used to this nowadays, so we've become blasé, but it's truly earth shattering for a world constructed around physical and political space. The death of distance may also be the death of barriers. On the Internet, nobody knows whether you are black, white, male, female, gay, or straight. We have the opportunity to build the secular society, to involve everyone. How many times have I wanted to buy goods from South Africa, the USA, or Australia, and had to wait until I visited the country? Now I can surf the net and someone in, say, Botswana can connect with me. That's good for me, of course, but it's also good for them. Everybody has the opportunity today to communicate; everybody has the opportunity to be someone. There are no 'isms'.

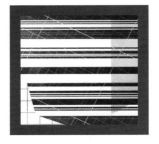

One of the biggest issues and challenges with the Internet is the danger that it is limited to those who have the wealth. You don't need to own a PC to get on the Internet but you do need to have the financial ability to buy access. So social exclusion is a danger. Governments should be making access for all a priority. Even in Britain, there are many people who are excluded from e-business. These tend to be immigrants, working-class people, and those who are less educated. Putting computers into schools is a critically important first step, of course. That builds awareness of the virtual world. But the advent of Internet cafés, and giving low- or no-cost entry, will build communities, which has real, positive benefits for the physical world.

But surely there are down sides? After all, bubbles always burst. We are at the outset of the electronic revolution and we need to remember that when we were at the outset of the Industrial Revolution, machines broke down. There was scepticism, failure, and despondency. The Industrial Revolution took 30 years to come into its own. The Internet is five years old and getting better by the day. Yesterday's leading edge is today's obsolescence. Life is moving at an extraordinary pace now, and the Internet is beginning to mirror this pace, not the other way around.

There is a healthy need for impatience; we cannot sit back and just allow the 'haves' to have alone. We are moving away from UK plc to Global Village plc. Who can argue with that as a successful strategy for mankind?

This is the most exciting time to be in the technology industry. Suddenly, we are not just delivering technology: we are changing lives. We are transforming businesses. We are breaking down barriers. How important does that make us? We have never had the opportunity before to create something so positive and enriching. What can be next?

This all seems tremendously altruistic

One could say that building and delivering an Internet business is the largest and most significant legal wealth creation mechanism that the world has ever seen. One of the major drivers behind the Internet is focusing on the time-poor, money-rich community, so it trades in instant gratification. The wealth creation for me is a means, not the end.

Fundamentally, all this isn't actually about e-business, the web, the Internet, and new technologies. It's about fast business. What the e-business world has generated are new rules of engagement. We have thrown away the necessity to have 20 years of experience before you become a director of your business. The focus now is on your imagination and courage as much as your expertise. Old slow business used to actively discourage diversity. Becoming a director meant setting out on a long journey with the aim to prove that you were 'one of us'. If you were seen to be sufficiently like us in mindset, values, behaviour, and dress code, you'd get the job – eventually. But fast business is inclusive of everyone. It is a merger of different skill sets, experiences, and learning to build a better world where the First World meets the Third World.

There is the need for care, but not caution. If we are brave we will be left with fast business that is the fusion of courage, imagination, enterprising companies, experience, and expertise.

The Internet is the home of diversity. My dream is that it will break down geographical, gender, and racial barriers. At last we have a real chance to promote difference: let's take it.

Are you
ready for turmoil?

Job title and company:
Managing Director, iSolon Ltd

Description of job:
iSolon is a web enabled business to business service providing experts and expertise to it's clients

Contact details:
www.iSolon.com or telephone
+ 44 (0)1353 662262

What are you most proud of?
My intuition

What do you remember most from your childhood?
My first and most powerful memory is of being in the womb and feeling very cramped. I have a fantastic memory that fortunately has stayed with me!

Who is your hero?
Nelson Mandela and others who sacrifice their personal freedom for a worthwhile cause.

Where is your favourite place in the world?
My own bed and my own bath.

Have you ever been in love and what did it feel like?
Once, it felt intense as though I were permanently on a high. It was surreal. Everything was magnified. It opened my understanding of me in relation to life. It also opened a huge gap that I had not been aware of. The emptiness all but consumed me. I think I could have fallen into that gap and disappeared forever.

What do you still want to achieve?
Inner peace

BEVERLY MANN

Are you ready for turmoil?

Wind gods

There is a corporate blackout. Organisations are groping their way through the Internet economy. In the darkness, despair, and panic, huge asteroids of information are eclipsing knowledge, resulting in a lack of insight and serious corporate pain. The whole process of company creation has changed irreversibly. There is no birth control in the Internet economy. Procreation and conception are not taking place in matrimonial boardrooms. The seeds of the new economy are being sown everywhere – in wine bars, on aeroplanes, in offices, bathrooms, and cyberspace – and germination is rapid. One day, people will ask you what it was like to live through the swerving 2000's as we crashed from one 'in ball' to another. The 'in ball' wizards of the new economy will conjure potions of magic and poison, and will create perfection and deformity. The power of the information gatekeeper will shrivel, and the wand of light will be held by knowledge experts whose beam can enlighten, transform and heal injured organisations. As the Internet economy heats up with the lava of competition, the very core of corporations will explode, making it dangerous to stay on the old corporate earth too long.

The early business pioneers will recognise that, although they are surrounded by route maps and information, there is no chartered path to the new galaxy, and even the most powerful of telescopes cannot vision it. Clever corporations will recognise that they cannot continually employ, train or maintain the degree of knowledge and expertise required for future navigation. Brave organisations will have prepared for an intergalactic voyage of discovery and will seek personal pilots to guide them through the interdimensional gateway and transport them to the new universe with its panoply of rising stars.

The new space explorer's transporter will be fuelled by highly classified experts with valuable, concentrated, hugely propelling knowledge vaults enabling a leap in time. Dwindling corporate oxygen will be consumed by the heavy breathers, still gasping that they have all the answers. As corporate oxygen reserves fail, ill-prepared executives will fight for survival suits. They will not be beamed up: they will be blasted away. The brave will prepare for the journey, the on-frequency people will pass through the interdimensional gateway, and the travelling companions will make the voyage of discovery fun and rewarding.

Are you ready for turmoil?

Brave organisations

Brave organisations will seek out wind gods to deliberately create turmoil and blow away old paradigms. The organisations that are calm before the storm are ill prepared to face the eye of the storm; those in turmoil will ride out the storm and emerge calm. The gods of wind will create irresistible forces of influence that will destroy prevailing conditions and give strength to the emerging breeze. The wind gods rarely reside within organisations; they are usually mavericks who cannot survive in the still air. Light breezes exist in organisations, but without wind gods they are unable to create the mass of velocity required to change existing practices. The wind gods will create ripples on the organisational millpond and fan the existing breeze, thus allowing the organisation to create its own wind tunnel where real testing of new-age travel can commence. The wind gods are experts in their own fields, not generalists masquerading as experts. They are capable of creating hurricanes, not puffs. Wind gods are viewed as wind-up merchants by organisational dragons that like to blow their own hot air. Are you brave enough to create a hurricane?

On frequency

If the majority of people within an organisation are not on the right frequency level, then they will not be able to listen to their colleagues that are. Lower frequency organisations will not be able to attract or keep beings that vibrate at higher levels. Without enough higher vibrating beings, the organisation will not be able to manifest the power needed to pass through the interdimensional gateway. Personal pilots will be sought to help an organisation steer to higher frequency levels.

Travelling companions

It is going to be a long journey to the new universal age. Why would you want to travel with boring companions who are going to annoy and frustrate you all the way? Surround yourself with travelling companions of like frequencies and hum along together. Several in-tune travelling companions will create powerful harmonies, making the journey fun and rewarding.

Job title and company:
Creative Director

Description of job:
Navigating with new thoughts and manipulating existing knowledge

Contact details: davidbirt@tgd.co.uk

What are you most proud of?
My daughters achievements (both)

What do you remember most from your childhood?
An unusual black & white shape, that changed from very thin to thick just before falling to sleep.

Who is your hero?
Don't have one.

Where is your favourite place in the world?
Haven't seen enough of it yet to decide.

Have you ever been in love and what did it feel like?
Still am! - Half a pair of scissors.

What do you still want to achieve?
Contentment

DAVID BIRT

Would you have like to have designed your own school?

Imagine

My dream is simple. I believe there are thousands of people out there doing things with their working lives that they find unfulfilling, frustrating, and boring. I suggest one of the reasons behind this torment is the education system that most kids experience.

Imagine that the goal of education and schooling was to identify and nurture the talents that lie in every individual, and to help shape a path for each individual that allows him or her to grow and excel with whatever gifts they possess, for the benefit of us all.

Education is driven by standards that tend towards conformity, not individuality, initiative or drawing the individual's capacity for enthusiasm. From an early age, this conformity tends to start indoctrinating young minds towards following the flow, fulfilling educational standards rather than becoming brilliant at the things they are best at. Individuality, initiative, and enthusiasm attached to a group of talents, identified and supported from an early age, create a powerful cocktail. Imagine the impact, both on the education system, and the future of our society. People would be good at what they are good at, providing meaningful work of value through which they could trade, rather than doing things just to get by.

I wonder what culture that dream would provide, and what qualities we should look for from the breeding grounds of our future?

The four calendar notes support the spirit of this dream – the dates are meaningless, the copylines timeless.

SEPTEMBER
MONDAY
23
One ounce of keenness is worth a whole library of certificates.

DECEMBER
FRIDAY
6
Failure is more frequently from want of energy than from want of capital.

AUGUST
THURSDAY
15
Be enthusiastic. It's the electricity of business.

OCTOBER
TUESDAY
22
The tree is known by its fruits; not by its roots.

PROCESS

INFORMATION TECHNOLOGY

FUTURE

DIGITAL AGE

MICROCHIP

010100110.101.0.01.01 .0.1.0.11

01. 001.01

FUTURE TECHNOLOGY

INFORMATION

01.01 .0.1.0.110.01.0.10. .0101.0.1

DVD

is it time for servants

to serve?

Job title and company:
TV Producer

Description of job:
Direct and produce investigative documentaries

What are you most proud of? My 10 year old Astra GTE

What do you remember most from your childhood? My cousin Will pushing my older brother into the fishing pond.

Who is your hero? My grandfather who played centre forward for Hendon FC.

Where is your favourite place in the world? The Cotton House, Mustique

Have you ever been in love and what did it feel like? Yes. Like the sweetest ever film edit.

What do you still want to achieve? A complete change of direction.

PHILIP EDWARDS

Is it time for servants to serve?

Wrestling power

My dream is drawn from Greek democracy. It is an idea designed to fundamentally combat the increasing autocracy of the workplace and the increasingly undemocratic nature of two-party politics.

The Greek city–state is the earliest and best example of pure democracy, where all citizens were involved in key decisions. Their democracy was known as direct democracy because every citizen was consulted directly on all legislation and asked to vote accordingly. The only flaws were that not everybody was a citizen and that the system was cumbersome to operate, hence the development of indirect democracy, with power mandated to elected representatives.

Unfortunately, indirect democracy has descended into farce with elected politicians tidying up their acts just before the next election, and comprehensively ignoring manifesto promises once in power. All this could change with the Internet.

My dream is that near-universal access of the Internet could be exploited to return democratic power to the electorate through Internet voting on key issues. Democratic e-votes could be counterbalanced by government votes to remove the possibility of cranky or extreme outcomes. The prospect of immediate feedback on behaviour would make politicians think more carefully before abandoning election commitments, and would restore flagging interest in stale and confrontational political parties.

A similar model would work in the workplace, involving both employees and shareholders. Voting could be used on decisions that affect the quality of life of staff and on company ethics, for example ethical sourcing, pension management, ethical investing, and redundancy policy.

This is not about cosy e-mail consultation groups but a real chance to wrestle back power from governments and boardrooms, and give it to the people with whom it should really lie. This is our best hope for continued world growth.

why are we in such a state

a state

0. 23 49 82 4 6

OC

SCAN

Job title and company: Chief Executive Officer, Care & Health.com

Description of job: Making everything happen

Contact details: mike.reid@careandhealth.co.uk

What are you most proud of? My friendships

What do you remember most from your childhood? Inequality in life

Who is your hero? Shakleton (not Geri Halliwell)

Where is your favourite place in the world? The Scottish west coast

Have you ever been in love and what did it feel like? Yes I have, it made me feel selfless.

What do you still want to achieve? Everything, I feel I've hardly started yet.

MICHAEL REID

Why are we in such a state?

Building choice into society

The Internet has sparked a revolution in how brands communicate trust with consumers. In a world that is being partially defined by increasing complexity of choice, it can be said that powerful brands are the beacons to guide consumers through this labyrinth. However, brands that fail to communicate trust will be ruthlessly exposed in this relentless transparent environment.

How does this explosion of information- and customer-centric behaviour from private sector brands sit with government's dealings with its citizens? What effect does the increasing difficulty of differentiation, now being experienced by private sector brands, have on government? How can government communicate trust, and define its brand? How do consumers want their accumulated tax payments, as represented by the finances of governments, to interact with them in providing the services that are currently defined as best produced by the traditional governmental model of aggregated removed choice?

Government would not need to exist in such a large state if we could all reliably conduct our own healthcare, build our own roads, and educate ourselves. Some activities that we deem as necessary have such long lead-time pay offs, or indeed pay off only if we to slip to the bottom rungs of society, but require the questionable benefits of the various implicit livelihood insurances that government provides to all citizens.

It can be said that one of the main roles of government is to aggregate, then implement, majority wishes. However, the consequence of this is that government is an intermediary between the payee and the service. In many industries, this has been proven to lead to poor quality of service, as the feedback loops of accountability lengthen and weaken. As one of government's major roles is to engage in a large-scale resource transfer between consumers and the excluded, how should it communicate to both sides, given the inherent weakness in the model? That is, to both the consumer providing the financial input, and the user, who increasingly is represented by the excluded. This is the current crucial quandary facing advanced democracies, where the growth of exclusion in society will increasingly be seen as a failure of the aggregation and provision model.

The definition of exclusion is the lack of opportunities that the rest of us take for granted. The prime philosophical point here is the increasing exercise of choice that the majority of society takes for granted and is exponentially engaged in providing and exercising. This is becoming the exclusionary principle. Choice in the private sector for most; no choice in the state economy for all of the rest. This is rapidly becoming the self-reinforcing debilitating scenario for the excluded.

As a generic brand, government is too large, varied, and structurally too unaccountable to accomplish the trust required to add true value. Capitalist societies denigrate governments as they attempt to shrink them. The preference setting is for government to justify its portion of national income, to be reinforced through removal at the polls. Removal, however, is a binary event, happening relatively infrequently. How can brand trust be built in this environment when, unlike with other brands, we play a direct role in its creation?

Looked at from this point of view, government could be the most trusted brand of all, and therefore be a consumer winner. There is a dramatic opportunity for improvement in its communications with its people from the growth of Internet penetration, allowing for shorter and faster feedback loops. All of this contributes to trust building.

Government is ultimately an expression of collected majority choices imposed among all. Since the Cold War, its overwhelming emphasis has been on national economic success. This has led to a return to an age of rationality, from a more ideological era. To express true differentiation in this field is a clear problem in the advanced democracies. As such, like all commodity producers, it has become the brand marketer's problem. How can we justify a product's continuing large role in society when it is starting to look as if it is at increasing odds with the rest of the economy?

To search the commercial world for a similar problem, we could turn to another market with differentiation issues, the household goods business, and ask: what differentiates the top three generic washing powders, and do they cater for all our laundry requirements? The answer is that they work for most of us, and few people can tell them apart. So, how do the brand promoters deal with this in an age of transparency? The answer is that they tend to compete on real segmentation that minority audiences require, or that they compete on price. OK, so how can we map this onto government's current role in a world where commodity, or undifferentiated products, are being forced down in price through free competition?

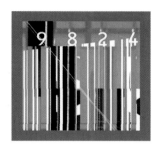

The direct comparison between soapsuds reacting to lack of differentiation by competing on price, and the role of government's increasingly undifferentiated product, may not seem clear. However, it is logical to postulate that if the direct aggregating and provisional role of government were to shrink to a less amorphous fragmented state, then consumers could identify more with the brand and in turn regain trust in it. That is to say, government must add value by being identifiable with consumers' individual needs, not merely a blanket agglomeration of services.

The increasing role of out-provision in giving government choice accomplishes part of this. It breaks continuous chains and presents opportunities for more focused minor alignments in each activity.

This increasing segmentation of roles allows stronger consumer identity with each point of aggregation and provision. Currently, this is being reflected in the creation of markets for many of its service provisions. These markets now touch many areas of provision, for example education, health, and social services.

The concept of government introducing choice for its own internal allocations is now broadly accepted. That is, where it spends or provides is now a semi-choice market. The challenge now is to carry this choice through to where consumers interact with government – the aggregation stage. Some of this has happened in a limited fashion in education, benefits, etc., but the true revolution is yet to happen.

By providers being focused on, first, providing choice to government and, second, providing direct choice to the people, feedback loops have been instituted. After all, an alternative as such is actually the beginning of a feedback loop. The economic success of providers will be related directly to their success in meeting consumer needs in a regulated framework.

Why are we in such a state?

The mechanism by which government can build brand trust deeper into the system is to increase sub-brands. The main brand is too diverse, ultimately too unaccountable to provide anything but the broadest identity. Sub-brand promotion, whether it is specific issues in local authorities, the NHS, or the environment, lowers the points of contact that citizens have with their service, and shortens feedback loops.

Very few advanced economies operate with shorter feedback than participation in the binary multi-year electoral cycle, but two exceptions spring to mind: California and Switzerland. Both have old, deeply ingrained democratic traditions. Both have used widely the specific referendum as a tool of policy. California, because it sees itself at the front of fresh-thinking human organisation and development; Switzerland because it has the tradition and compactness to accomplish this regularly.

The Internet is now going to make propagation of both these shorter and more specific feedback loops possible throughout the democratic world. It will reduce the spread between how government and the private sector act, to a point where government is

compelled to reinvent itself, and remove the disabling parts of its brand to replace with the enabling. Implicitly in the middle of all this, it will be educating all of its citizens in modern formats of thought that incorporate choice through the mechanisms of its interactions. This, crucially, is the point at which government respects human nature and allows all its citizens, excluded or not, to participate in a society of choice. This is how it can enable and exploit the strengths of a brand that we all create and belong to.

Job title and company: Director, Simmons Gallery

Description of job: Dealer in historical coins, medals, weights and related material; contemporary sculpture, medals and jewellery. Organiser of the London Coin Fair.

Contact details: Simmons Gallery, 53 Lambs Conduit Street, Bloomsbury, London WC1N 3NB Tel: 020 7831 2080 Fax 020 7831 2090 www.simmonsgallery.co.uk

What are you most proud of? Creating a business and a family at the same time.

What do you remember most from your childhood? Books, and dreaming of visiting all those places I read about.

Who is your hero? My very cheerful and talented piano teacher; she was all joy and fortitude, and great fun. And Bette Midler for being so outrageous.

Where is your favourite place in the world? Too many to choose from but home and our gallery come tops.

Have you ever been in love and what did it feel like? Yes. But why use the past tense?

What do you still want to achieve? Even more harmony and riches.

FRANCES & HOWARD SIMMONS

Have you started living your dream?

Discipline and enthusiasm

When Howard and I first decided to deal in coins and medals back in 1982, we could see what computers might do for our business: delivering information rapidly and selectively, helping us to provide an individually tailored service for specialist collectors. The core part of our business, then and now, is matching individual coins, medals, tokens, anything to do with money or the way it is made, historical or contemporary, with key collectors. But being a tiny operation – and a trading one – all our money originally needed to go into buying and selling coins and medals. It's a niche market, and since we opened Simmons Gallery in Holborn, we've got a further speciality, being the only gallery in the UK to promote the contemporary art medal.

We couldn't afford the advanced technology when we started – only the largest corporations could do that. Our first computer had the power of our son's pocket money diary today. There was no fax, no Internet, no scanners, no digital photography. Sending images meant photography and a series of processes, each one getting further away from the object. We just had to wait for the technology to come within our economic reach.

Since August 1999, we have had a website that we use as a virtual illustrated catalogue and general news-sheet. It needs updating regularly, and there are certain sections that I know I really should refresh. A mixture of discipline and enthusiasm for the latest acquisition is what's needed here. We post details of the current exhibition in the gallery, and our auction catalogue. We receive about 50 directly useful e-mails every week, and a virtual in-tray seems so much less daunting than a stack of papers. No paper, address, envelope or stamp to find. Just think, write, and click, and it's done.

Have you started living your dream?

Now we can scan a coin, send it as an e-mail attachment to a collector in Germany, and he has the information he needs to decide whether or not to buy. The condition and variety of the piece is all there to see in colour. An e-mailed reply keeps it for the collector until his next visit to London.

In a business relationship built up over many years, the most rewarding part of selling is meeting our customers face to face and allowing them to handle the coin or the medal they're buying. The great pleasure gained from this type of collecting is the combination of the visual, the tactile, and the intellectual. It only occurs when you have a bronze or coin in your hand, feel the weight of it, see the skill with which it was made, looking first at one side and then the other, seeing how they relate.

This is the point where we find limitations to the Internet and the real reason why we need a gallery, a place to meet people, rather than just working in an office, and selling by mail order or via the Internet.

And how do we manage distribution across borders? The price of postage and couriers is increasing. There are customs regulations, problems with security, and insurance to arrange. None of these is becoming easier for us. Instead, our customers tell us to keep the piece until they visit us.

SIMON RHIND-TUTT

Are you heading for the dunce's corner?

Efficiency versus effectiveness

There's a lot of talk these days about how the Internet is changing our lives. Everything can be done quicker, leaving us all more time to spend more time with our families or having fun. That's the theory, anyway. The reality, though, is a bit different.

What the Internet, and convergence of technology generally, has done is to shift the weight of everybody's expectations. People have already come to expect that because things can be done quicker, then more can be done overall.

The irony is that in the high-tech world of the new millennium, the adage coined in the early 20th century to describe the British civil service (known as Parkinson's Law) that 'work expands to fill the time available for its completion' has never been truer. There's another side to the development of digital technology, which causes some concern – the tendency to resort to electronic means of communication for all purposes. The trouble is, electronic communication isn't always the most appropriate for the job in hand.

An e-mail may not give the whole picture. A simple phrase such as 'Fine – go ahead' can be easily misconstrued in an e-mail. Say the phrase out loud and it could mean that someone is not buying into your idea but is apathetic enough to let it go, or that the person is eager to let you push the idea forward; it could even represent challenge or threat.

E-mail has its place and conveys the hard facts, but it doesn't give any soft information. A face-to-face meeting can be so much more revealing – body language can speak volumes, and can expose how people really feel, irrespective of what they are saying. Enlightened businesses will recognise the efficiency of what the Internet can bring, but still value personal dialogue and recognise where and when it has a place.

It's no surprise that recruitment consultants who have flirted with the Internet as a means of reviewing CVs have reintroduced personal meetings as a way of ensuring fit between candidate and client needs.

A brave new world where everything is done online, and personal interaction and relationship building are relegated to options to be selected on a drop-down menu, is the ultimate nightmare. We must ensure that the generation that has grown up on pagers, mobile phones, e-mail and (soon) WAP are not consigned to the 'dunce's corner' when it comes to knowing how to build effective, personal relationships. After all, being more efficient doesn't necessarily mean being more effective.

ROBIN HUNT

Job title and company: Creative Director, arehaus

Description of job: Being Creative

Contact details: robin@arehaus.com

What are you most proud of? My father, arehaus

What do you remember most from your childhood? The balloon that crash-landed in our cottage garden in Kent. And the offer (which wasn't taken up) to crew for a summer in Chamonix with the ballooning team I brought in for breakfast aged 16. The fact I didn't go still haunts me – who would I be now if I'd gone?

Who is your hero? I have hundreds of heroes in my life: today some would include Walter Gropius, Raymond Chandler, F Scott Fitzgerald, Tim Berners-Lee, Ben Bradlee, Juliette Greco, Miles Davis, Antonio Carlos Jobim, Saul Bass, William Thackeray, Rachel Whiteread, Piet Mondrian, Philip Cavendish, Goya, Jackson Pollock, Harry Palmer, James Bond and Roger O. Thornhill.

Where is your favourite place in the world? Ushuia in Tierra del Fuego (on the Beagle Canal), Manhattan (anywhere)

Have you ever been in love and what did it feel like? Yes, terrible.

What do you still want to achieve? To be in love and it not feel terrible. To create lasting work in a time of light-speed change.

How do you create your very best things?

Skirting around vertigo

The essence of vertigo is a feeling of illusionary movement. It may manifest in a variety of sensations such as light-headedness, fainting, spinning, or dizziness. The symptoms are usually due to a disturbance of vestibular system within the inner ear.

'Skirting Around Vertigo', the only object of art that hangs in my minimal home, was commissioned for an exhibition that took place in London in the autumn of 1999. Thirty artists, designers, and fashion folk were invited by the design company, Skirt, to create a piece of work inspired by the phrase 'a bit of skirt'.

There were the inevitable images of supermodels in short things and not much more; there was a Posh-and-Becks dress; there were art installations involving old records and video machines. But my favourite piece, a deceptively simple photograph, was created by my friend, the designer Friederike Huber.

'Skirting Around Vertigo' is composed of two photographic images. That on the left-hand side is a formal, vertiginous picture of the back stairs at the Swiss Centre cinema in London. In the other image, beneath an arch in grey-black shadow, a faintly drawn Spaniard in matador outfit introduces himself to a woman in a rich scarlet dress.

Brought together initially by tone and colour, the two images are strangely complementary, the picture's title an added allusion. The stair image is angular and confusing: it could have been photographed looking downwards from the fourth storey, or it could be a tower or some steps photographed and framed horizontally from within some unknown darkened room. The striking red banister rail and the warmer, flash-lit rail above it both lead the eye upwards, though we know they both, in fact, take visitors to the cinema downwards towards the exit. The other image, which shares the balance of creamy light, the shock of red, the dark, foreboding shadowing, is sensual and hand-drawn, a dreamy blur of real red material creating the illusion of the woman's skirt, the lightness of touch in the illustration taking us away from the formality of the architecture to our left. Some kind of male/female exchange is taking place here in this image; some kind of balancing is taking place overall.

We begin to think about *Vertigo*, Alfred Hitchcock's masterpiece. *Vertigo* is a film that has inspired shelves of analyses: its themes include those of memory, guilt and control; the balance of the sensual and the rational, the male and female, Catholicism and capitalism. It is a film, in the end, about the dream like dizziness we all feel confronted with in life: confronted with things we don't fully understand.

In the film, San Francisco police detective Scottie Ferguson, played with all the battered, confused Everyman quality that only James Stewart can give, develops a fear of heights and is forced to retire when a colleague falls to his death during a chase Stewart is leading. In retirement, wandering aimlessly and single, he is hired by an old college friend to follow his wife, Madeleine, played with a blurry luminosity by Kim Novak. Madeleine has become obsessed with a painting of a mysterious Spanish woman from the 19th century that hangs in the local museum. Scottie's friend is fearful for his wife; he believes her to be suicidal and unhinged. As the labyrinths of plot unravel, like the rings of an ancient Redwood tree, not only does Scottie learn about Madeleine, but he also leans more of the vertigo that comes from heights, and from the heights of passion and obsession. He learns about deception and trust; he learns about the power of the unconscious.

Friederike's art piece alludes to many of these things: primarily the balance of the rational and the sensual, and the unconscious pleasure we find when these two elements are in some way united. I think often about many of these themes looking at the picture, but often in utterly different contexts. The left-hand side represents, sometimes, the confusing vertigo brought on by work. How do we look at work? As something to be always striving upwards for? As something to be fearful of when we have reached a certain height? As something that is always impossible to fully comprehend – darkness and light at the same time? Is there a sexual symbolism in this image that reminds us of glass ceilings, of the potency of money, of the career ladder (Jacob's ladder?), of the fact that we, in business, are always – despite the expensive consultants we hire – looking through a glass?

It reminds me how often we can be passionate fools about work, obsessed, mistrustful or too trusting, in the same way that we can about love. It reminds me of the way work and business can define us, make formal our striving for a grand narrative – my work is my life, and all that. How the business plan is everything, or how the great invention is. It reminds me of how infrequently the balance of all things is achieved. How infrequently we look even from two directions at the same time.

The right-hand image alludes to the things for which business should have no part: escape, heat and sun, romance, mystery – above all, light and passion. Yet, as we know from life, and from *Vertigo*, the balance of these two sides is often skewed. *Vertigo* is a film of profound romantic cynicism in some ways; read another way, it is testament to the power of the unconscious to take us beyond the everyday, to make us dream. 'Skirting Around Vertigo' juxtaposes these two ideas and asks us to respond.

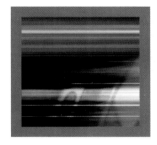

At one stage in the film, Kim Novak's *Madeleine* – or it could be the woman in red in this image, for notice how here the man is a cipher, just as Scottie is in *Vertigo* – tells the besotted James Stewart: 'Only one is a wanderer; two together are always going somewhere.' It is true also in this image: the formal structure and the sensual moment combine to create a piece of art going somewhere.

The essence of true vertigo is a feeling of illusionary movement, I discover from the web this morning. That 'illusionary movement' is present in this work, and with us at those moments when the very best things are created. For vertigo is not something to be frightened of. Skirting around vertigo, at the very least, means that we are still alive to something new. That we are going somewhere, even if we are not sure where.

Robin Hunt is the Creative Director of arehaus, the new media design consultancy. He is the co-author of *Retailisation*, which is soon to be published.

Job title and company:

Managing Director - Sense Worldwide

Description of job:

Seeing – Doing - Learning

Contact details:

www.senseworldwide.com or www.museum.uk.com [another interesting operation]

JEREMY BROWN

What are you most proud of?

My Friends

What do you remember most from your childhood?

Being Different

Who is your hero:

Siddhartha

Where is your favourite place in the world?

My Home

Have you ever been in love and what did it feel like?

Yes, I love it.

What do you still want to achieve?

Kung Fu prowess

ABOVE THE LINE – c.1986

'TV IS NOT THE ONLY FRUIT'

I'VE GOT A NEW BRAND

GREAT – LET'S PUT IT ON TV

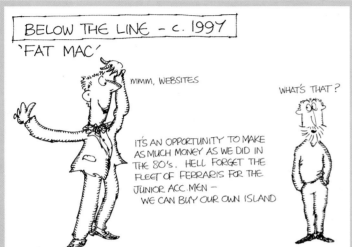

IT'S A WRAP

Conclusion

What is the conclusion?

There is no conclusion.

But there is a way forward.

Hopefully, having read *Brand Storm* you will want to take action using the *Brand Storm* diagnostics to prepare you and your organisation for the Human Economy. I think it is impossible to over-estimate the opportunity facing us but crucially it is equally impossible to over-estimate the expectations of the Human Economy customer.

Maybe you've read *Brand Storm* cover to cover, maybe you've just dipped in and out, whichever way, *Brand Storm* should not be a one-off experience. Try out some of the actions. Refer to the Ideas to develop your thinking anew. Keep checking your progress along the way using the Actions. And throughout the whole process never forget to keep dreaming.

Dream big.

And set your service standards higher than you can dream.

Good Storming.

I look forward to learning from your experiences. Keep in touch.

Will Murray

will.murray@brandstorm.com

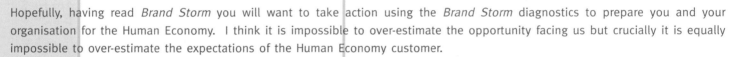

CREDITS

Brand Storm has been brought to you by Will Murray and Financial Times Prentice Hall, in association with Bora Marketing Communications Ltd.

Director – Will Murray

Executive Producer – Richard Stagg

Producer – Jacqueline Cassidy

Art Director – David Turner

Designer – David Stimson

Cameraman – Keith Powditch

Illustrator – Geoff Norman

Model – Caroline Turner

Dancers – Gemma Mulcock, Rachel Stanley & Lara Goddard

Special Effects Director – Kevin Wolff

Screenwriter – Sarah Heathcote

Best girls – Helen Baxter, Emma Carr

Gaffer – Geoff Chatterton

Publicists – Sarah Harper, Michela Rossi

 **Bora Marketing Communications**

Technicolor provided by Bora Marketing Communications Ltd.
01793 838300   www.bora.co.uk

David

David

Keith

Geoff

Caroline

THE TEAM

When we set out to produce *Brand Storm* all we had was a vague idea in our minds of what we wanted the book to look like.

It is only because everyone involved contributed so many ideas, that the *Brand Storm* book you now see has come alive.